A NEW CHRIST-CENTERED ADAPTATION OF THE MOST
SUCCESSFUL APPROACH TO RECOVERY EVER DEVISED

RAPHA'S 12-STEP PROGRAM FOR

OVERCOMING CHEMICAL DEPENDENCY

ROBERT S. McGEE

RAPHA'S TWELVE-STEP PROGRAM
FOR OVERCOMING CHEMICAL DEPENDENCY

with support materials from *The Search for Significance*

Robert S. McGee

Robert S. McGee
Publishing

mcgeepublishing.com
800.460.4673

Rapha's Twelve-Step Program for Overcoming Chemical Dependency
By Robert S. McGee

Scripture quotations are from the New American Standard Bible, copyright, The Lockman Foundation 1960, 1962, 1963, 1971, 1972, 1973, 1975, 1977.

The Twelve Steps have been reprinted and adapted with permission from Alcoholics Anonymous World Services, Inc., to extend to all persons suffering from chemical dependency, and to credit the One whom we believe is our source of power: Jesus Christ.

Portions of *The Search for Significance* book and workbook have been reprinted and adapted with permission of the author.

Rapha's Twelve-Step Program for Overcoming Chemical Dependency represents the experiences and opinions of Rapha and the authors. Opinions expressed herein are not to be attributed to Alcoholics Anonymous as a whole, nor does *Rapha's Twelve-Step Program for Overcoming Chemical Dependency* imply any endorsement by Alcoholics Anonymous.

Fourteenth Printing, Second Edition, 1996
ISBN: 0-945276-10-9
Printed in the United States of America

Contents

Step One

We admit that by ourselves we are powerless over chemical substances – that our lives have become unmanageable. *For I know that nothing good dwells in me, that is, in my flesh; for the wishing is present in me, but the doing of the good is not* (Rom. 7:18).

Step Two

We come to believe that God, through Jesus Christ, can restore us to sanity. *For it is God, who is at work in you, both to will and to work for His good pleasure* (Phil. 2:13).

Step Three

We make a decision to turn our lives over to God through Jesus Christ. *I urge you therefore, brethren by the mercies of God, to present your bodies a living and holy sacrifice, acceptable to God, which is your spiritual service of worship* (Rom. 12:1).

Step Four

We make a searching and fearless moral inventory of ourselves. *Let us examine and prove our ways, and let us return to the Lord* (Lam.3: 40).

Step Five

We admit to God, to ourselves, and to another human being the exact nature of our wrongs. *Therefore, confess your sins to one another, and pray for one another, so that you may be healed* (James 5:16a).

Step Six

We commit ourselves to obedience to God, desiring that He remove patterns of sin from our lives. *Humble yourselves in the presence of the Lord, and He will exalt you* (James 4:10).

Step Seven

We humbly ask God to renew our minds so that our sinful patterns can be transformed into patterns of righteousness. *And do not be conformed to this world, but be transformed by the renewing of your mind, that you may prove what the will of God is, that which is good and acceptable and perfect* (Rom. 12:2).

Step Eight   **127**

We make a list of all persons we have harmed, and become willing to make amends to them all. *And just as you want men to treat you, treat them in the same way* (Luke 6:31).

Step Nine   **137**

We make direct amends to such people where possible, except when doing so will injure them or others. *If therefore you are presenting your offering at the altar, and there remember that your brother has something against you, leave your offering there before the altar, and go your way; first be reconciled to your brother, and then come and present your offering* (Matt. 5:23-24).

Step Ten   **140**

We continue to take personal inventory, and when we are wrong, promptly admit it. *Therefore let him who thinks he stands take heed lest he fall* (1 Cor. 10:12).

Step Eleven   **150**

We seek to grow in our relationship with Jesus Christ through prayer, meditation, and obedience, praying for wisdom and power to carry out His will. *But if any of you lacks wisdom, let him ask of God, who gives to all men generously and without reproach, and it will be given to him. But let him asks in faith without any doubting, for the one who doubts is like the surf of the sea driven and tossed by the wind* (James 1:5-6)

Step Twelve   **164**

Having had a spiritual awakening, we try to carry the message of Christ's grace and restoration power to others who are chemically dependent, and to practice these principles in all of our affairs. *Brethren, even if a man is caught in any trespass, you who are spiritual, restore such a one in a spirit of gentleness; each one looking to yourself, lest you too be tempted.* (Gal. 6:1).

Notes   **170**

Introduction

No one, in charting the course of his future, makes plans to become chemically dependent. Addiction is usually the last thing on a person's mind when he takes his first drink or experiences his first high. Instead, he is most often thinking about being accepted by his peers, and about the glamour and excitement he perceives drinking or drugging will bring him.

If he gets hooked, the exuberance of his early association with alcohol or drugs will fade as the years pass. His drug of choice will become a reward for hard work, a remedy for anger, a means of controlling other people, a boost for his energy level, an escape from pain, a substitute for companionship, a self-prescribed aid to depression. His habit will become a need, and as it progresses, his life will begin to crumble. His drug of choice will no longer bring him a sense of freedom, but bondage, isolation, anxiety, fear, and shame. He may experience broken relationships, the loss of a job, financial failure, declining health, and a deteriorating self-esteem. Sadly, he (of all people) may be the last to see his addiction. Without help, he will probably die.

Why do people become chemically dependent? No one is really sure. What is known is that in addition to a complex interaction of cultural, environmental, interpersonal, intrapersonal, and biological factors, the body of an addict cannot process alcohol or drugs normally. The presence of any chemical substance alters the cells in his nervous system, resulting in a craving for the substance, and withdrawal symptoms when it is taken away.[i]

It is estimated that one in every ten persons becomes chemically dependent, and that these people cannot stop drinking or using by themselves. While it does happen, it is generally a myth that the addict will have enough insight to see his condition and seek treatment for it.[2] It is also a myth to assume that addiction favors those on skid row. In actuality, only five percent of those who are chemically dependent live on skid row.[3]

Understanding these facts may enable you to see that addiction is very commonplace in society, and can happen to folks just like us, regardless of our reputation, social standing, or religious beliefs.

If you are chemically dependent, you're in great company. And we mean *great*! Some of the world's strongest leaders – in their country, community, or business – have been where you are now. Their problems weren't solved in a day, a week, or even a year, but they have made great progress in their lives because they've had an opportunity to work a Twelve-Step program. You see, our work, in recovery is not just deliverance from alcohol or drugs. Our work is deliverance from unhealthy patterns of behavior before and after we started drinking or using.

Rapha's Twelve-Step Program for Overcoming Chemical Dependency is designed to facilitate that deliverance and to complement the original, biblically-based Twelve Steps of Alcoholics Anonymous. Our workbook contains questions and studies to help you understand why you think and act as you do. Based on our experience with others, we are convinced that a deep application of biblical truth over a period of time can bring profound and lasting change to your life. For this reason, we refer to the steps outlined here as steps of *progress*. Progress is our goal in recovery, not perfection.

Stages of Addiction

The downward spiral of addiction usually follows a predictable cycle which includes experimenting and learning, seeking, obsessing, and consuming. Let's look at some of the characteristics of each of these stages:

Stage One: Experimenting and Learning
In this stage, the user....

- Receives encouragement to try alcohol or drugs from peers, counselor, dental or medical practitioner
- Personally desires to be accepted and/or to escape, modify, or avoid pain – emotional and/or physical
- Typically uses "light stuff" (alcohol, marijuana), though may occasionally use hard drugs
- Experiences euphoric effects of alcohol and/or drugs, usually with few consequences for using or drinking behavior
- Learns to trust chemical substance and its effects, and learns that those effects are controlled by amount of intake.

Stage Two: Seeking
Having learned that alcohol/drugs will produce "good" feelings, the user...

- Uses alcohol/drugs "socially"
- Establishes limits for drinking/using ("Two drinks are my limit." "I only take my medication as directed." "I never take a drink until after my kids are in bed and the day's responsibilities are over."
- May use alcohol/drugs to excess occasionally and experience hangovers, blackouts, or other physical manifestations of overdoing
- Can usually continue to control the amount of alcohol/drugs he or she uses
- May experience disruption in regular work or school activities as a result of drinking/using
- Generally feels no emotional pain for choice to drink or use

Stage Three: Obsessing
Alcohol/drugs become important, and in this stage, the user...

- Becomes preoccupied with getting "high"
- Develops compulsive approach to using/drinking
- Begins to experience periodic loss of control over alcohol/drug use
- Breaks self-imposed rules about substance use established in stage 2, and increases drinking/using times and quantities
- Loses sense of self-worth, and instead begins to feel guilt and shame for behaviors when high

- Projects self-hatred onto others as health, emotional stability, interpersonal relationships, and fellowship with God are adversely affected by using/drinking
- Begins to rationalize, justify, and minimize negative feelings about himself or herself.

Stage Four: Consuming
The substance "has" the user, and now he or she…

- Must use alcohol/drugs just to feel "normal"
- Believes other people and circumstances are the root of his or her problems
- May entertain thoughts of additional escape possibilities such as suicide, leaving his or her family, moving out of town, etc.
- Experiences deteriorating physical health, as well as mental, spiritual, and emotional health
- Continually feels guilt, shame, remorse, anxiety, paranoia
- Experiences withdrawal symptoms

How can we begin the process for effective, lasting change? The answer begins with the following six components:

A   Admit
N   New Start
S   Support group
W   Willingness
E   Education
R   Relapse prevention

Let's examine each of these elements of recovery:

Admit

Admitting powerlessness over the compulsion to get drunk or high is the first crucial step of recovery. Why? Because we're not apt to invest ourselves fully in something we don't believe in, and staying clean and sober requires the kind of energy that must be backed by conviction.

As necessary as it is, and as obvious as it may seem to others, an admission of addiction usually comes slowly for the dependent person. The reason behind this is that chemical dependency evolves from abusing alcohol and/or drugs to meet one's needs for comfort and esteem. In many cases, getting drunk or high begins as a mood-altering experiment which progresses to a repetitious coping mechanism for "getting along" with life. This is because chemical substances produce feelings of euphoria, especially the early stages of use. As the pleasure centers of the brain "learn" this effect, impulses to use or drink will gradually exceed the logic for not using of drinking. Defense mechanisms such as denial and repression sabotage decisions to quit. Finally, the user or drinker is addicted when the substance alters his or her brain chemistry so that the drug becomes vital to its normal functioning.

These are some of the reasons why no amount of logic or willpower can defeat chemical addition until the dependent person is placed in a supportive care environment. This may include detoxification, inpatient or outpatient treatment, or daily attendance at support group meetings with a new routine which revolves around abstinence from substance use – all depending on the severity of one's addiction.

If you are having trouble seeing and understanding the harmful effects of your addiction, be patient with yourself as you work through step one. Obviously, you are entering recovery because you or someone else thinks you need to be. Still, it takes time to develop objectivity and an open-minded attitude about something which has been perceived as necessary for one's well-being for some time.

New Start

As we attempt to break free from a life-threatening habit, we have the opportunity for a new start in life. Developing some new, constructive habits in place of those that have proven to be self-defeating enhances our self-esteem. Habits that could contribute to our new start might be changing the route we take to work, to school, or home; varying our routine when we get up, come home, or get ready for bed; making new friends, perhaps with people who will contribute toward our recovery rather than our dependency.

We may need to seek out a more accurate concept of God, and place ourselves in situations where we can experience His love, forgiveness, and strength. A better understanding of His character and motives for us usually helps us to gain a new attitude about accepting others and sharing ourselves with them.

Support Groups

Personal reflection and application are most effective in an environment of affirmation and encouragement. This may include individual therapy, but you also need the support of others who have gone through (or are going through) this program of healing. This is especially important! It is extremely difficult – if not impossible – overcome the painful causes and effects of addiction alone. Often, those closest to us (though they mean well) have learned that our repeated promises to stop drinking or using mean nothing. They now may be understandably dubious that this time, we mean business. It will also take time for them to adjust to your new behavior. Those who have been where you are now understand. Let them help you!

Willingness

If your recovery is dependent on anything, it may be the degree of your willingness to get and stay clean or sober. To be willing is to be ready to act voluntarily. It is an attitude in action which says, *I'll do anything,* and then does just that.

In recovery, *anything* might be working through a twelve-step program; attending a support group meeting on a daily basis for the first ninety days of recovery, or admitting oneself to a structured inpatient or outpatient treatment program. *Anything* may mean gradually allowing other people to become involved in one's life; being completely honest with oneself and others; considering a personal relationship with God; learning how to tolerate those people one would normally criticize.

Of course, you may be entering recovery completely against your will. You may have no desire to stop drinking or using because you have yet to see the need to do so. Give yourself some time. More importantly, give yourself an opportunity to cultivate the kind of willingness that will do *anything* to get better by investing yourself in a program of recovery.

Education

In many ways, recovery is simply a learning process about life and how to live it. To choose "real life" is to choose the experiences of joy and sorrow, love and grief, need and want, contentment and peace, victory and defeat.

If we're new to recovery, chances are that we know little about living "real life." Learning how to respond to life in a healthy way requires some education about our addiction to chemical substances: why we started drinking or using and how our addiction has affected us and others. Perhaps of the most immediate value is learning what triggers your compulsion to drink or use now. When do you especially want to get drunk or high, and why? Educating yourself with the answers to these questions will prolong your life!

As you grow in recovery, you will have opportunities to discover your emotions. It may now be difficult for you to differentiate between anger and grief, or love and affection. In time, however, you will gain a better understanding of your feelings and a greater appreciation for them.

With recovery comes an almost immediate awareness of needing people as never before. Interaction contributes to the satisfaction we sought unsuccessfully through drinking or using. In time, we will be able to embrace what we need to learn about building and enjoying healthy relationships.

Gradually, we also will learn that we choose our behaviors, and that every choice we make produces either a positive or a negative result.

As we grow, we will learn how to assume responsibility for our behavior, rather than allowing ourselves to be controlled by something or someone else.

Living in reality, we also will have an opportunity to learn more about God and to compare our new knowledge with our old conceptions about Him.

Of course, none of this can be learned in a day, or a week, or even a year. Perhaps one of the most valuable things we can begin teaching ourselves right now is to be patient while we're learning. Again, all of recovery is a learning process…it will take a lifetime to educate ourselves about productive ways of living and how to put that knowledge into practice.

Relapse Prevention

Studies show that 80 percent of those who enter recovery relapse within the first ninety days. This is primarily because people in recovery fail to develop new strategies for handling life's problems. How can one prevent relapse? Let's look at the principles:

☐ *Warning Signs*
Look for signals that your commitment to recovery is slipping:
• Is your attendance at recovery group meetings waning?

- Are you actively participating in group meetings as well as a twelve-step program of recovery?
- Who are you spending your time with: people who reinforce your recovery, or people who could influence you to resume drinking or using?
- Are you having feelings of deflated self-worth or omnipotence?
- Do you find yourself criticizing or blaming others?
- Are you acting defensively toward others?
- Have you started to experiment again?

☐ *Accountability*

- Are you placing yourself in an environment where you are open about your anxieties, doubts, and fears?
- Are you allowing others to ask you hard questions?
- Are you avoiding persons who care about your recovery, such as your spouse, counselor, sponsor, or pastor?

☐ *Don't Give Up*

Heeding the warning signs will help you stay on the path of recovery. Remaining in relationships and situations which offer accountability will strengthen and protect you. Ask for help if you need it – your recovery is truly a matter of life and death.

Note: For more information about relapse, see the material under "The Road to Relapse" at the end of step 2.

Recovery is a process. Lasting change won't occur overnight. You may experience flashes of insight occasionally, but the process of real growth is long, slow, and steady. Be patient. Work through the exercises carefully. Growth and health will come.

As you practice these "steps of progress," your behavior will gradually begin to change. But more importantly, your understanding of yourself, your concept of God, and your relationships with others will improve, providing a strong foundation for a lasting recovery, and a healthy and productive life.

God be with you.

God declares that the church (those who have accepted Christ as Lord and Savior) are to be about setting captives free. This means you need to have some Christians praying against the power of darkness, specifically in the life of the addicted.

This does not mean they will not have to make choices but the consistent faithful prayers will make these choices happen with less interference from the forces of evil.

Do not worry about having an organization (i.e. a local organized church); do this, but having a few true believers praying for the addicted person will make a world of difference.

STEP ONE

We admit that by ourselves we are powerless over chemical substances – that
Our lives have become unmanageable.

For I know that nothing good dwells in me, that is, in my flesh;
for the wishing is present in me, but the doing of the good is not. (Rom. 7:18)

Addiction wears many faces; it has no respect for a person's age, race, sex, social standing, profession, or religious belief. Some seem to be genetically predisposed to chemical addiction, and are "hooked" with the first drink, puff, or pill. Others may abuse chemical substances for a number of years before crossing the line to dependency.

Either way, the distinguishing mark of addiction is **powerlessness.** Initially, this may be difficult to grasp because the effect triggered by chemical substances is usually – with prolonged use – one of control. We *think* we are in control when we are drinking or using. We are apt to feel out of control only when our drug of choice has been taken away and our comfort level begins to plummet. In reality, the sense of control we gain from drinking of using is a misconception.

There are usually two types of active addicts: those who know they are powerless over their dependency but cannot stop drinking or using, and those who cannot yet see their powerlessness over chemical substances.

One reason for this inability to recognize signs of powerlessness is the nature of drugs themselves. Chemical substances act on the central nervous system to produce feelings of euphoria, a lack of inhibitions, and a sense of well-being. Some of these substances are accurately labeled *pain killers.* They not only deaden physical pain, but cross the emotional boundaries and deaden emotional pain as well. More often than not, the person suffering from chemical dependency is also suffering from such pain. Part of this is a result of the fact that his life, because of addiction, has become **unmanageable**. In an effort to block pain, the addict has built elaborately structured defense mechanisms which also prevent his seeing the truth about his addiction. This *denial,* combined with the numbing effects of chemical substances, makes it very difficult to perceive reality as it is.

By the time he becomes involved in treatment, the chemically dependent person usually knows he is hurting, and he may want help. But usually, he isn't able or willing to recognize his dependency as the culprit for his unhappy situation. Instead, he blames his boss or his parents, his spouse or his children, his circumstances or God. When he arrives at treatment, it is often with the idea that if he can get *these* people and/or circumstances straightened out, life will again be comfortable and he can continue drinking or using happily ever after.

Before you can hope to make any progress or feel any better, it is essential to examine your own life for signs of **powerlessness** and **unmanageability** as a result of chemical dependency. Moving forward is usually preceded by looking backward; before we can adequately deal with the present, we must examine our past.

Powerlessness

Answer the following questions as accurately as possible:

☐ What kinds of drugs, including alcohol, have you used in your lifetime?

☐ When did you first begin using drugs?
- Alcohol?
- Why?
- Why do you think you have continued to use them?

☐ How often have you used drugs?
- Alcohol?

☐ In what amounts have you used drugs, including alcohol?

☐ Do you think your answers to the above questions indicate "normal" usage, i.e., like the rest of society?

☐ Have you ever experienced loss of memory, dulled vision, or loss of consciousness as a result of using or drinking?

☐ Have you ever tried to control your consumption of chemicals or alcohol?
- If so, why?
- Were you able to do this easily?

☐ Estimate how often you usually think about using chemicals or alcohol:

☐ Prior to treatment, how much of your time was usually spent on some aspect of drinking or using; for example, obtaining, using, and recuperating from alcohol or drugs?

☐ How has *powerlessness* over your chemical/alcohol usage become evident to you?

Unmanageability

☐ What does *unmanageability* mean to you?

☐ What is your current physical condition (blood pressure, ulcers, stamina, ability to sleep well, heart, liver, kidneys, chronic diarrhea, etc.)?

☐ Could your physical condition stem from previously unmanageable behavior?

☐ What feelings have you tried to alter or ignore through chemical substances or alcohol?

☐ Describe any mood swings or unpredictable behaviors that have resulted from using alcohol or chemicals:

☐ Have you ever experienced negative physical or emotional symptoms as a result of not drinking or using? These might include nausea, vomiting, feeling especially weak or prone to illness, elevated blood pressure, unexplained sweating, depressed mood, anxiety, irritability, headaches, hallucinations, insomnia. Describe any of these feelings in your:

☐ How has your use of chemicals or alcohol been destructive to you?
• How has it been destructive to others (e.g. accidents, dangerous situations, physical or verbal abuse, etc.)?

☐ Name five ways chemicals and/or alcohol have led you to compromise your values:

☐ Name five ways chemicals and/or alcohol have contributed to financial, occupational, or legal problems in your life:

☐ What crises have resulted in your life from using chemicals and/or alcohol?

☐ What crisis brought you into treatment? (Describe in detail):

Symptoms of Chemical Dependency

The past several pages have given you an opportunity to reflect on your behavior as it relates to your previous experiences with alcohol and/or drugs. Now we'll examine symptoms associated with chemical dependency.

By definition, *chemical dependency* is the compulsion (forceful urge) to drink and/or use a chemical substance to achieve a desired effect, despite the experience of negative consequences for doing so. *Codependency* is the condition occurring when a person's God-given needs for love and security have been blocked in a relationship with a dysfunctional (dependent) person, resulting in a lack of objectivity, a warped sense of responsibility, being controlled and controlling others, hurt and anger, guilt and loneliness.[1] Codependents often perpetuate addictive behavior by rescuing the dependent person from the consequences of his or her addiction. In a number of instances, individuals exhibit both chemically dependent and codependent behavior. Typically, persons who exhibit *three* of the following symptoms for a month's duration, or repeatedly over a longer period of time, are classified as chemically dependent.[2] These symptoms are:

1. Using a substance in larger amounts or over a longer period of time than originally intended.
2. Demonstrating an inability to reduce or control substance use, despite one's desire to stop or cut back.
3. Spending large amounts of time in activities revolving around substance use, i.e. in obtaining, using, and recuperating from the effects of the substance.
4. Being intoxified or suffering from withdrawal when expected to fulfill important obligations (work, school, home), or in situations when substance use is hazardous to oneself and/or others (driving, piloting, operating machinery).
5. Giving up or avoiding important social, occupational, or recreational activities to drink or use.
6. Continuing to drink or use after recognizing that substance use is contributing to one's physical, psychological, relational, financial, occupational, or legal problems.
7. Taking increasingly larger amounts of a substance to achieve the same desired effect.
8. Experiencing withdrawal symptoms upon cessation or reduced intake of the substance.
9. Resuming or increasing substance use to relieve or avoid withdrawal symptoms.

Are you addicted to chemical substances?

Stages of Acceptance

Despite the negative symptoms, consequences, and complications of addiction, and the many benefits associated with recovery, many chemically dependent persons report profound feelings of loss at the onset of sobriety. Though these feelings eventually decline in frequency and intensity, they may last from several weeks to several years, depending on the severity of addition.

One author has identified five stages experienced by those who are terminally ill.[3] Our observations have confirmed that those withdrawing from substance addiction usually pass through similar phases at various intervals during the recovery process:

Denial: Most chemically dependent persons are unable or unwilling to acknowledge their addiction – to themselves or others – despite obvious signs that they and their loved ones are suffering as a result of it.

David was a dentist with a fifteen-year addiction to Demerol and codeine. When he lost his house, he blamed his wife. When his wife left him, he blamed his practice. When he lost his license, he blamed God, "who's had it out for me since the beginning." David was confronted several times about his drug problem. "Problem? What problem? I've just had a rough go of things," he said. Sadly, David remained unconvinced of his dependency. He eventually acquired AIDS as a result of using contaminated needles.

Bargaining: Bargaining usually marks the beginning of the dependent person's recognition of his or her addiction, and is an attempt to postpone quitting. Bargaining can occur with oneself: "I need to kick this, but I'm just too restless right now. What's one more Valium? I'll quit later." Or, it can be a response to others: "Of course I'm still serious about quitting, and I will – right after this project at work blows over." Or, it can be a plea to God: "God, help me stop – tomorrow."

Anger: When the chemically dependent person can no longer escape the facts pointing to his or her addiction, and/or when he or she finally enters treatment, anger is a normal response. Frequent objects of anger are God, family members, or close friends, all of whom – according to the dependent person – contributed to his or her addiction or entry to treatment. His or her anger may also be directed toward others who are drinking or using (jealousy); the circumstances of needing to enter recovery; and anger with himself or herself for perpetuating this perceived tragedy and for feeling helpless to overcome it alone.

Grief: The majority of chemically dependent persons have become experts at avoiding painful emotions. The experience of deep distress, or grief, during recovery is often an unwelcome surprise.

Many of us associate grief with the loss of a loved one, but feelings of grief are a normal response to the loss of anything we might consider important to our well-being.

Substance abuse often provides an immediate payoff: It may calm one's nerves; block feelings of pain, failure, or disappointment; or give one a sense of euphoria, courage, power, or control. In addition, because the cycle of addition turns one increasingly inward, chemical substances often become a primary means of support. When this "support" is taken away, it is like losing a good friend. Grieving over such a loss is normal, healthy aspect of recovery (even though it does not feel good), and is done properly when one gives himself or herself the freedom to feel loss whenever he or she is reminded of it.

Acceptance: Over time, those who continue in recovery are able to accept their addiction and their need for treatment. Most are gradually able to accept a life apart from alcohol and/or drugs with serenity, and eventually, joy.

□ These stages often overlap in actual experience. Which one(s) are you in now? Describe your present feelings:

Recovery is a *process*. It is not like taking a pill or having a drink and then suddenly feeling better. Recovery is actually far more satisfying than that, and leads to a contentment and peace within that is *lasting.*

Along the way, you may discover that your addiction is a combination of different problems, but you will also have the satisfaction of seeing many of the problems that developed as a result of chemical abuse subside. Again, this will take time. Be patient with yourself. Be patient with those around you may not be used to your new patterns of behavior. But above all, continue with the process. It really *is* worth it!

For Additional Reflection and Application

□ Read Ps. 20:2-3; 51:17; 116:1-9; 147:10-11. Why does admitting weakness to God give Him an opportunity to strengthen us?

□ Read Is. 55:8-9; Jer. 9:23-24; Rom. 7:18-20; 2 Cor. 1:9; 3:4-5. Why is it important to place our trust in God, rather than in ourselves?

□ Read 2 Cor. 12:9-10 and Heb. 11:32-34. What comfort and encouragement do you find in being "weak" before God?

□ Read Eph. 3:14-21, and in the space below, write what you most need from God right now, using this passage to guide you.

STEP TWO

We come to believe that God, through Jesus Christ, can restore us to sanity.

For it is God who is at work in you, both to will and to work for His good pleasure. (Phil. 2:13)

For many of those who are chemically dependent, step 2 often presents two hurdles: one is often God, and the other is the issue of "sanity" which, in this step, may seem to imply that those who are chemically dependent are lacking in it. Because it is essential to understand our need for healing before we can turn to the Healer for help, we will examine "sanity" first.

Sanity

While it is true that prolonged abuse of chemical substances can lead to personality changes and mental illness, *sanity*, in this step, has the same meaning as that used in *Webster's New World Dictionary:* "soundness of judgment."

The ability to reason declines markedly when the chemically dependent person is drinking or using, whether he or she is high or not.

Some examples of the insanity which accompanies addiction include:

- Drinking or using despite warnings of deteriorating health
- Drinking or using despite the pain it causes others
- Drinking or using in retaliation against someone who has offended us or made us angry
- Drinking or using to prove we can "handle it," despite our experience that we can't
- Cutting ourselves off from friends, family members, or anyone else who attempts to interfere with our drinking or drug abuse
- Changing or canceling appointments or commitments to make time for drinking or using
- Blaming other people for both our behavior and our inability to handle chemical substances
- Insisting that we are somehow "different" from other people who are addicted to chemical substances
- Drinking or using despite threats of loss (job, home, spouse) if we continue
- Drinking or using when it places us and/or others in jeopardy
- Getting close to success in any area of life, and then "blowing it" with an alcohol or drug binge
- Drinking or using despite our earnest desire to stop

The *insanity* is that chemically dependent persons continually reap the consequences of their actions for drinking or drugging – at an accelerated rate as their addiction progresses – and yet, for a long time, no price is so high that they are willing to stop.

☐ Using the examples on the previous page as a guide, list five occasions when you have acted in such a way that an objective observer, who knows you and your circumstances, might say, "That's *insane*!"

Complications in Your View of God

If talking about God makes you feel uncomfortable, that's perfectly understandable. By the time the chemically dependent person arrives for treatment, his concept of God is usually fairly negative. He may have had a faulty perception of God since childhood and long before his history of chemical usage; however, repetitious substance abuse has further clouded his perception, extinguishing most – if not all – of his spiritual understanding.

Another complication in the dependent person's relationship with God is *guilt*. Perhaps he feels guilty for his drug abuse. More likely, he feels guilty for what he did while drinking and/or using.

Chemical substances and alcohol go to work on the central nervous system, releasing inhibitions and implanting feelings of euphoria. When inhibitions are released, a person's values often go with them. A man or woman who would never consciously plan to be unfaithful to his or her spouse might crawl into bed with a perfect stranger under the influence of alcohol or drugs. Or, to protect himself and his drug or alcohol supply, the dependent person may resort to stealing or lying. These are just a few examples; the bottom line, however, is guilt.

☐ How would you describe feelings of guilt?

☐ Do you feel guilty; do you block the pain of guilt by denying that you've done anything wrong, or both? Explain:

☐ How has guilt and/or denial affected:
- Your self-esteem?
- Your relationship with your family?
- Your relationships with others?
- Your relationship with God?

19

Still another obstacle in the dependent person's relationship with God is *blame*. As his addiction progresses, the addict becomes increasingly preoccupied with his "habit," always wondering when he's going to be able to drink or use again, and how he's going to feel if he does or does not get high. As a result, his focus is continually turned inward, toward himself. Self therefore becomes his most precious commodity, and protecting himself, his greatest priority. This self-protective behavior may be compounded by a low self-esteem. The addict may have suffered from a poor self-image prior to drinking; in fact, it may have been his low sense of self-worth that initially triggered this "escapist" behavior. Add to this his oppressive burden of guilt and shame for what he's done either to get high or while he is high, and the result is deep self-hatred.

The chemically dependent person projects this self-hatred onto other people by blaming them either instead of himself or in addition to himself. He blames others because he truly believes that they (and he) should get what is deserved. He blames others because his success may depend on their contributions, and when they fail, it makes him look bad. Putting someone else down may temporarily make him feel better about himself.

Blame is often the result of unmet expectations. By blaming someone who fails, we often feel superior. In fact, the higher the position of the one who fails (parent, boss, pastor, etc.), the farther they fall, and the better we feel. What higher authority can the dependent person blame than God?

☐ How do you respond when you fail?

☐ How do you respond to others when they fail?

☐ List the various ways that we condemn others (observable, unobservable, verbal, nonverbal behaviors):

- Which of the above do you use & how do you use it?

☐ Do you blame God? If so, describe how and why:

☐ Do you feel that God is condemning of you? If so, describe how and why:

20

"*Come* to Believe..."

Because of these and other complications in the chemically dependent person's relationship with God, it is important to note that step 2 states that we "*come* to believe." This is a process. Spiritual giants are not born that way. It often takes time, some understanding, and experience before our faith in God actually begins to take root and grow. Here, it is also important to realize that it is not the *quantity* of our faith, but the *quality* of our faith that counts most with God.

Whether you believe any of the above obstacles are true of you or not, if you are feeling distant from God, know that no one plans to force Him on you. Rather, our intent is to present you with an opportunity to examine your perceptions of Him and correct any that you may find faulty.

Your Parents and You

Our view of God, our self-concept, and our ability to relate to others are primarily shaped by our parental relationships. If our parents were loving and supportive, we will probably believe that God is loving and strong. If, however, our parents were harsh and demanding, we will probably believe that God is impossible to please. Either way, the foundation of our emotional, relational, and spiritual health is usually established by parental modeling, and the results can be wonderful or tragic.[1]

In order to gain a better understanding of this "shaping" process, it is helpful to examine the characteristics of our parents and our relationship with them.

The following is an exercise to help you evaluate your relationship with your father as you were growing up.[2] Check the appropriate squares as you recall how he related to you when you were young. Here is an example:

EXAMPLE:

Characteristics	Always	Very often	Some-times	Hardly Ever	Never	Don't Know
Gentle			√			
Stern	√					
Loving			√			
Aloof			√			
Disapproving		√				
Distant	√					

WHEN I WAS A CHILD, MY FATHER WAS...

Characteristics	Always	Very Often	Sometimes	Hardly Ever	Never	Don't Know
Gentle						
Stern						
Loving						
Aloof						
Disapproving						
Distant						
Close and Intimate						
Kind						
Angry						
Caring						
Demanding						
Supportive						
Interested						
Discipliner						
Gracious						
Harsh						
Wise						
Holy						
Leader						
Provider						
Trustworthy						
Joyful						
Forgiving						
Good						
Cherishing of Me						
Compassionate						
Impatient						
Unreasonable						
Strong						
Protective						
Passive						
Encouraging						
Sensitive						
Just						
Unpredictable						

Evaluation of Your Relationship with Your Father

☐ What does this inventory tell you about your relationship with your father?

☐ If you were an objective observer of the type of relationship you have just described, how would you describe your father?

☐ How would you think the child would be affected by this relationship?

Now complete the same exercise, this time to evaluate your relationship with your mother: [3]

WHEN I WAS A CHILD, MY MOTHER WAS...

Characteristics	Always	Very Often	Sometimes	Hardly Ever	Never	Don't Know
Gentle						
Stern						
Loving						
Aloof						
Disapproving						
Distant						
Close and Intimate						
Kind						
Angry						
Caring						
Demanding						
Supportive						
Interested						
Discipliner						
Gracious						
Harsh						
Wise						
Holy						
Leader						
Provider						
Trustworthy						
Joyful						
Forgiving						
Good						
Cherishing of Me						
Compassionate						
Impatient						
Unreasonable						
Strong						
Protective						
Passive						
Encouraging						
Sensitive						
Just						
Unpredictable						

Evaluation of Your Relationship with Your Mother

☐ What does this inventory tell you about your relationship with your mother?

☐ If you were an objective observer of the type of relationship you have just described, how would you describe your mother?

☐ How would you think the child would be affected by this relationship?

Evaluating Your Relationship with God

We can begin to see how our relationships with our parents have influenced our perception of god when we evaluate our present relationship with Him. The following inventory will help you to determine some of your feelings toward God.[4] Because it is subjective, there are no right or wrong answers. To ensure that the test reveals your actual feelings, please follow the instructions carefully.

- Answer openly and honestly. Don't respond from a theological knowledge of God, but from personal experience.
- Don't describe what the relationship *ought* to be, or what you *hope* it will be, but what it is right now.
- Some people feel God might be displeased if they give a negative answer. Nothing is further from the truth. He is pleased with our honesty. A foundation of transparency is required for growth to occur.
- Turn each characteristic into a question. For example: *To what degree do I really feel that God loves me? To what degree do I really feel that God understands me?*

25

TO WHAT DEGREE DO I REALLY FEEL GOD IS...

Characteristics	Always	Very Often	Sometimes	Hardly Ever	Never	Don't Know
Gentle						
Stern						
Loving						
Aloof						
Disapproving						
Distant						
Close and Intimate						
Kind						
Angry						
Caring						
Demanding						
Supportive						
Interested						
Discipliner						
Gracious						
Harsh						
Wise						
Holy						
Leader						
Provider						
Trustworthy						
Joyful						
Forgiving						
Good						
Cherishing of Me						
Compassionate						
Impatient						
Unreasonable						
Strong						
Protective						
Passive						
Encouraging						
Sensitive						
Just						
Unpredictable						

☐ What does this exercise tell you about your relationship with God?

☐ Are there any differences between what you know (theologically) and how you feel (emotionally) about Him? If so, what are they?

Your Father's Influence on Your Relationship with God

Now that we have examined your current relationship with God, let's look at how your relationship with your earthly father has influenced your perception of your heavenly Father.[5]

To make a comparison, transfer all of the check marks you made for your own father on page 22 to the *shaded* columns on page 28. When you have completed this, transfer the check marks you made on page 26 which relate to your relationship with God. To make them more obvious, use an "X" for this category.

EXAMPLE:

Characteristics	Always		Very often		Some-times		Hardly Ever		Never		Don't Know	
Gentle				X	X							
Stern	X			X								
Loving				X	X							
Aloof					X			X				
Disapproving			X					X				

27

Instructions: Transfer all check marks from page 22 to the SHADED columns. Transfer all check marks from page 26 to the WHITE columns.

Characteristics	Always		Very often		Some-times		Hardly Ever		Never		Don't Know	
Gentle												
Stern												
Loving												
Aloof												
Disapproving												
Distant												
Close and Intimate												
Kind												
Angry												
Caring												
Demanding												
Interested												
Disciplinal												
Gracious												
Harsh												
Wise												
Holy												
Leader												
Provident												
Trustworthy												
Joyful												
Forgiving												
Good												
Cherishing of Me												
Compassionate												
Impatient												
Unreasonable												
Strong												
Protective												
Passive												
Encouraging												
Sensitive												
Just												
Unpredictable												

☐ Which characteristics are the same for both your father and your heavenly Father?

☐ Which characteristics are quite different (two or more boxes away from each other)?

☐ What patterns (if any) do you see?

☐ How has your perception of God been shaped by your relationship with your father?

Your Mother's Influence on Your Relationship with God

How has your mother influenced your perception of your heavenly Father?[6] To get a comparison, transfer all the check marks you made for your mother on page 24 to the columns on the following table. Use a check mark for this category.

When you have completed this, transfer the check marks you made on page 26, which relate to your relationship with God. To make this obvious, use an "X" for this category. Put them in the appropriate columns on the following table.

EXAMPLE:

Characteristics	Always	Very often	Some-times	Hardly Ever	Never	Don't Know
Gentle		X	X			
Stern	X	X				
Loving		X	X			
Aloof			X	X		
Disapproving	X			X		

Instructions: Transfer all check marks from page 24 to the SHADED columns. Transfer all check marks from page 26 to the WHITE columns.

Characteristics	Always		Very often		Some- times		Hardly Ever		Never		Don't Know	
Gentle												
Stern												
Loving												
Aloof												
Disapproving												
Distant												
Close and Intimate												
Kind												
Angry												
Caring												
Demanding												
Interested												
Disciplinal												
Gracious												
Harsh												
Wise												
Holy												
Leader												
Provident												
Trustworthy												
Joyful												
Forgiving												
Good												
Cherishing of Me												
Compassionate												
Impatient												
Unreasonable												
Strong												
Protective												
Passive												
Encouraging												

☐ Which characteristics are the same for both your mother and your heavenly Father?

☐ Which characteristics are quite different (two or more boxes away from each other)?

☐ What patterns (if any) do you see?

☐ How has your perception of God been shaped by your relationship with your mother?

Learning More About God from Psalm 139

Some passages in Scripture highlight certain aspects of our relationship with God. Psalm 139 is a perfect example of this because it describes the character of God in a number of ways. Studying it can help you understand how His *omniscience* (being all knowing), *omnipresence* (being ever present), and *omnipotence* (being all powerful) can apply to you and your circumstances.

We will examine a few verses from this psalm at a time. Then we will ask questions to promote reflection.[7]

God Knows Me Thoroughly

Verses 1-4 (NIV): *O Lord, you have searched me and you know me. You know when I sit and when I rise; you perceive my thoughts from afar. You discern my going out and my lying down; you are familiar with all my ways. Before a word is on my tongue you know it completely, O Lord.*

☐ God always knows everything about you. You can keep no secrets from Him, yet He loves you unconditionally! How does this make you feel?

☐ In what ways does God's omniscience give you courage and strength?

He Protects Me

Verses 5-6 (NIV): You *hem me in – behind and before; you have laid your hand upon me. Such knowledge is too wonderful for me, too lofty for me to attain.*

☐ God's perfect knowledge about you enables Him to protect you (to hem you in). From what do you need His protection?

☐ Is it difficult for you to understand the Lord's omniscience? Why, or why not?

He Is Always Present

Verses 7-12 (NIV): Where can I go from your Spirit? Where can I flee from your presence? If I go up to the heavens, you are there; if I make my bed in the depths (Hebrew Sheol), you are there. If I rise on the wings of the dawn, if I settle on the far side of the sea, even there your hand will guide me, your right hand will hold me fast. If I say, "Surely the darkness will hide me and the light become night around me," even the darkness will not be dark to you; the night will shine like the day, for darkness is as light to you.

☐ The most important assurance to one who has strayed is that he is not lost! How close is God to you?

☐ How close does He seem to be?

☐ How far can you get from Him?

He Is a Sovereign Creator

Verses 13-15 (NIV): For you created my inmost being; you knit me together in my mother's womb. I praise you because I am fearfully and wonderfully made; your works are wonderful, I know that full well. My frame was not hidden from you when I was made in the secret place. When I was woven together in the depths of the earth...

☐ Who is responsible for the creation of your body?

• Do you believe that the One who created you can also restore you? If so, why?

• Can you rejoice that you look exactly the way the Father wants you to look? If so, why?

• If not, why not?

• How do you normally respond to your appearance?

• How does your perception of your appearance affect your self-image?

☐ Do you think (or worry) about what other people think of your appearance? Why, or why not?

☐ How could this psalm help free you from the fear of what others think of you?

God Has a Plan for You

Verse 16 (NIV): *Your eyes saw my unformed body. All the days ordained for me were written in your book before one of them came to be.*

☐ Describe any comfort you gain from knowing that God has a plan for your life:

☐ What types of plans do you suppose God might have for your life?

Examples:

He wants me to have a relationship with Him through His Son, Jesus Christ (John 3:16-18).
He wants to provide for my welfare, and give me a future and a hope (Jer. 29:11)
He wants to give me things that will be good for me (Matt. 7:7-11).
He wants to strengthen me (Is. 40:29).
He wants me to spend eternity with Him (John 14:1-3).

God Is Constant and Consistent

Verses 17,18 (NIV): *How precious to me are your thoughts, O God! How vast is the sum of them! Were I to count them, they would outnumber the grains of sand. When I awake, I am still with you.*

☐ The Lord is infinite and He is thinking about you all the time! How does that fact comfort and encourage you?

Our Response

Verses 23-24 (NIV): *Search me, O God, and know my heart; test me and know my anxious thoughts. See if there is any offensive way in me, and lead me in the way everlasting.*

Openness to God's correction and guidance is the way the psalmist responds to the secure position he has with God. You also can have a secure position with God, through Jesus Christ, who died to pay for your sins and rose from the dead to give you new life.

☐ Are you open to God's correction and guidance?
• Why, or why not?

For Additional Reflection and Application

☐ Read Matt. 9:12-13.

- What comfort does this passage give you?
- Do you believe that God, through Jesus Christ, can restore you to "sanity"?

☐ Read Mark 9:23-24.

- If you do not believe that God can restore you to "sanity," how can you follow the father's example in this passage?
- Are you willing to ask God to help you in your unbelief?

Belief Systems

By completing this step, you are on your way to becoming familiar with both your perception of God and what Scripture tells us about His ways. Understanding the truth of God's Word is the beginning of our restoration. Throughout the four gospels, Jesus repeatedly emphasized the importance of *believing* Him, Why? Because our actions are usually based on our beliefs!

The book, *The Search for Significance*, by Robert S, McGee, identifies four false beliefs which distort our perception of both God and ourselves. All of these lies are based on the primary belief that our **self-worth = performance + other's opinions.** In other words, we suffer from a misconception that our significance, or worth, is determined by what we do and what others think of us. Each of these four false beliefs (listed below) results in a specific fear:

False Belief: *I must meet certain standards to feel good about myself. If I fail to meet these standards, I cannot really feel good about myself.* This belief results in the **fear of failure.**

False Belief: *I must be approved (accepted) by certain people to accept myself. If I do not have the approval of these people, I cannot accept myself.* This belief results in the **fear of rejection.**

False Belief: Those *who fail are unworthy of love and deserve to be blamed and condemned.* This belief leads to the **fear of punishment and the propensity to punish others.**

False Belief: I *am what I am. I cannot change. I am hopeless. This means I am simply a total of all my past performances, both good and bad. I am what I have done.* This belief leads to a **sense of shame.**

For each of these false beliefs, there is a corresponding truth from God's Word, the Scriptures:

Satan's Lie **Your worth = Your performance plus other's opinions**	God's Truth **Your worth = What God says about you**
I must meet certain standards to feel good about myself. If I don't...(Fear of Failure)	Justification (Rom. 3:19-25; 2Cor. 5:21): *I am completely forgiven and fully pleasing to God.*
I must be approved (accepted) by certain others to feel good about myself. If I'm not approved... (Fear of Rejection)	Reconciliation (Col. 1:19-22): *I am totally accepted (by God).*
Those who fail are unworthy of love and deserve to be blamed and condemned... (Fear of punishment/ Punishing Others)	Propitiation (1 John 4:9-11): *I am deeply loved (by God).*
I am what I am; I cannot change; I am hopeless (Shame)	Regeneration (2 Cor. 5:17): *I am absolutely complete in Christ.*

Renewing our perception of God, ourselves, and others by changing our belief system will take time, study, and experience. It has taken years to develop patterns of behavior that reflects a false belief system. It will take time to change. We will continue to examine these beliefs throughout this workbook. The process of learning to apply God's truth to our lives may be painful at times, but it is also rich, rewarding, and exciting!

The Road to Relapse

Before moving to step 3, it is important to learn something about relapse. *Relapse* is returning to alcohol or drugs after a period of abstinence. Relapse is a possibility for anyone in recovery, regardless of how long he or she has been clean or sober. The reason this is true is because even though one has stopped drinking or using, he or she has not stopped having addictive personality. When that addictive personality begins to control the recovering person's life, he or she is said to be a "dry drunk," one who has sobriety, but no serenity. In fact, the recovering person may exhibit all of the behaviors associated with his or her using or drinking days – without the presence of chemical substances.

__Warning Signals__

Like recovery, relapse is a process comprised of behaviors, attitudes, feelings, and thoughts which culminate in drinking or using. One may fall into a relapse over a period of hours, days, weeks, or even months.

Warning signals to alert you to a possible relapse are:

- Feeling uneasy, afraid, and anxious, sometimes about staying clean or sober. This begins to increase as "serenity" decreases.
- Ignore feelings of fear and anxiety, and refusing to talk about them with others.
- Having a low tolerance for frustration.
- Becoming defiant, so that rebelliousness begins to replace what has been love and acceptance. Anger becomes one's ruling emotion.
- The "ISM" (I-self-me) attitude grows. Self-centered behavior begins to rule one's attitudes and feelings.
- Increasing dishonesty, whereby small lies begin to surface as deceptive thinking again takes over.
- Increased isolation and withdrawal characterized by missing groups and withdrawing from friends, family, and support.
- Exhibiting a critical, judgmental attitude, a behavior which is often a process of projection as the group member feels shame and guilt for his or her own negative behaviors.
- Overconfidence manifested by statements such as, "I'll never drink (or use) again," or by simply believing that one is the "exception" to all rules about recovery. He does not need to come to meetings anymore. She can handle going back to the old friends and places.
- Underconfidence about oneself manifested by self-derogatory remarks, overwhelming feelings of failure, a tendency to set oneself up for a failure.

Special Stressors

In addition to these warning signals, it is important to be alert to certain times which can make one more vulnerable to relapse. Some of these include:

- Completing the first week of sobriety
- Completing the first twenty-one days of sobriety, and any anniversaries for sobriety thereafter, specifically: ninety days, six months, nine months, one year
- Holidays
- Personal anniversaries, birthdays, or other special days
- Experiencing "high" moods of exuberance, perhaps after receiving a raise, getting a job, getting engaged or married, etc. (Many people fail to realize that "high" moods are as stressful as low moods.)
- Becoming overly hungry, angry, lonely, or tired

☐ Do you see any of your attitudes and actions in the above warning signals? If so, list and describe them:
- With whom can you talk about these attitudes and/or actions?
- What actions do you need to consider taking to avert these signals?

Resisting Urges

Experiencing the urge to drink or use again is a normal part of recovery. The intensity and frequency of these urges depends on the severity of one's addiction, and often differs with each person. It is important to be alert to those things which might trigger a compelling urge to drink or use again.

These might include specific associations typically made with drinking or using: eating certain foods, spending time in certain restaurants or bars, listening to some types of music or particular songs, being involved in certain types of festivities, such as outdoor lake parties or barbecues. You may simply see someone drinking a beer on his way home from work, and suddenly feel a strong urge to have a drink.

The above are outer triggers for drinking or using; however, we also need too be alert about what we're feeling on the inside which may prompt us to drink or use. Some examples might be feeling angry, distressed, overwhelmed, pressured to meet a deadline, jealous of others who seem able to drink or use.

Finally, it's wise to be aware of certain attitudes that can trigger a return to drinking or using, such as: *It's not fair that I can't drink or use,* or, *I sure could handle a lot more pressure when I was using,* or, *I sure felt a lot smarter when I was drinking,* or, *I can't face this crisis without getting high!*

☐ Think of times when you have experienced a strong desire to drink or use. Describe one of those situations as best as you can recall it.

• What outer triggers or associations prompted your urge to drink or use?

• What inner feelings were you experiencing at the time?

• What were some of your attitudes about recovery, about yourself, and about others?

• What steps did you take to overcome your desire to drink or use?

• Try to think of five steps you can take in the future when you feel a strong urge to drink or use, and list those in the spaces below:

Practicing Relapse Prevention

Preventing relapse is learned, just as all new behaviors in recovery are learned over a period of time. To help you practice relapse prevention, we suggest you look over the following list at the conclusion of each day to see how you're doing:

• Do you recognize any warning signals that you need to heed?
• Did you experience any compelling urges to drink or use?

☐ If you answered yes to either of these questions, what specific action can you take to eliminate a possible relapse?

STEP THREE

We make a decision to turn our lives over to God through Jesus Christ.

I urge you, therefore, brethren, by the mercies of God, to present your bodies a living and holy sacrifice, acceptable to God, which is your spiritual service of worship. (Rom. 12:1)

In step 2, we acknowledged that God, in His infinite greatness, can restore us to *sanity.* In step 3, we choose to turn our lives over to His care so that we can begin to experience that restoration process.

This is not just a one-time step. For the person following God, submitting to Him is a daily (or hourly!) choice (see Josh. 24:15). There are probably a few of us who relish the concept of being submissive in any kind of relationship, but Scripture says we will become slaves of that which we obey (Rom. 6:16). In the case of chemical dependency, we have a choice: to submit to our compulsion and allow it to direct our lives as before, or to submit to God and allow Him to be a source of new direction for us.

God knows that we will only follow one whom we know and trust (1 John 10:3-5). Our purpose in writing this step is to help you build upon your knowledge of God and understand why He is trustworthy. At the same time, we also want to equip you with an understanding of why man has a tendency to refuse God's help and trust instead in himself.

The Fall of Man
The Old Testament depicts the original incident of sin and the Fall of Man:

When the woman saw that the tree was good for food, and that it was a delight to the eyes, and that the tree was desirable to make one wise, she took from its fruit and ate; and she gave also to her husband with her, and he ate.
Then the eyes of both of them were opened, and they knew that they were naked; and they sewed fig leaves together and made themselves loin coverings. (Gen. 3:6-7)

To understand the devastating effects of this event properly, we need to examine the nature of man prior to sin. Adam, the first created man, was complete and perfectly made in the image of God (Gen. 1:27). His purpose was to reflect God's glory; to demonstrate His holiness (Ps. 99:3-5); love and patience (1 Cor. 13:4); forbearance (1 Cor. 13:7); wisdom (James 3:13,17); comfort (2 Cor. 1:3-4); forgiveness (Heb. 10:17); faithfulness (Ps. 89:1,2,5,8); and grace (Ps.111: 4).

Adam was God's most important creation. To meet his needs for companionship and understanding, God created a woman for Adam and gave her to him as his wife. So great was His approval of this couple that He blessed them so that they could bear children, and commanded them to *fill the earth, and subdue it; and rule over the fish of the sea and over the birds of the sky, and over every living thing that moves on the earth* (Gen. 1:28).

Then, God planted a garden in an area called Eden, which means "delight" (Gen. 2:8), and which was surrounded by an abundance of resources. These include *every tree that is pleasing to the sight and good for food* (Gen. 2:9); a river that was the source of the Tigris and the Euphrates (Gen. 2:10-15); and gold, bdellium, and onyx (Gen. 2:12). Here, God placed Adam and his wife to cultivate the garden and keep it (Gen. 2:15). To satisfy their spiritual needs, God visited Adam and Eve and talked with them personally.

Adam and Eve were perfect in body, mind, and spirit. Scripture indicates that they were surrounded by a perfect environment and free to enjoy all that was in it, with one exception:

And the Lord God commanded the man, saying, "From any tree of the garden you may eat freely;
*but from the tree of the knowledge of good and evil you shall not eat, for in the day that you eat from it you shall surely die." (*Gen. 2:16-17)

Like Adam and Eve, Satan also was created in perfection. At the time of his creation, his name was Lucifer, which means "morning star." He was an angel of the highest rank, created to glorify God. Sadly, Lucifer's pride caused him to rebel against God, and he was cast from heaven with a third of the angels (Is. 14:12-15). When he appeared to Adam and Eve in the garden it was in the form of a serpent, *more crafty than any beast of the field which the Lord God had made* (Gen. 3:1).

Although Adam had been given authority over the earth, if he, like Lucifer, rebelled against God, he would lose both his authority and perfection. He would become a slave to Satan and to sin (Rom. 6:17), and a child of God's wrath (Eph. 2:3). Therefore, destroying man was Satan's way to reign on earth and, he apparently thought, to thwart God's glorious plan for man.

To accomplish this goal, Satan deceived Eve, who fell to the temptation. Eve ate of the tree of the knowledge of good and evil, believing it would make her wise and like God. Adam, however, was not deceived. He deliberately chose to forsake the love and security of God and follow Eve in sin. Paul explained this fact to Timothy:

And it was not Adam who was deceived, but the woman being quite deceived, fell into transgression. (1 Tim. 2:14)

In doing this, Adam lost the glory of God had intended for mankind, and forfeited his close fellowship with God. Adam's deliberate rebellion also aided Satan's purpose, giving him power and authority on earth. From that moment on, all history led to a single hill outside of Jerusalem, where God appointed a Savior to pay for man's sin of rebellion.

Though we justly deserve God's wrath because of that deliberate rebellion (our attempts to find security and purpose apart from Him), His Son became our substitute, experienced the wrath our rebellion deserves, and paid the penalty for our sins. Christ's death is the most overwhelming evidence of God's love for us. Because Christ paid for our sins, our relationship with God has been restored, and we are able to partake of His nature and character, to commune with Him, and to reflect His love to all the world.

Let's look at the characteristics of Christ that we begin to experience when we place our trust in Him.

Characteristics of Christ

The following study is designed to help you develop a better understanding of Christ's character through Scripture.[1] To help you think through each passage and consider what it means, we want you to paraphrase each passage in the space provided. The goal is not to "fill in the blanks," but to reflect on what these passages are saying. This will take some time. Be thorough with this exercise, and think both about the meaning of each passage, and how to apply it in your daily experience.

Purpose

When Adam sinned, he brought both the burden and the penalty of sin upon all mankind. As a result, man is by nature rebellious against God, separated from Him, and deserving of His righteous wrath.

Behold, the Lord's hand is not so short that it cannot save; neither is His ear so dull that it cannot hear.

But your iniquities have made a separation between you and your God, and your sins have hidden His face from you, so that He does not hear. (Is. 59:1-2)

- Paraphrase:

Or do you think lightly of the riches of His kindness and forbearance and patience, not knowing that the kindness of God leads you to repentance?

But because of your stubbornness and unrepentant heart you are storing up wrath for yourself in the day of wrath and revelation of the righteous judgment of God... (Rom. 2:4-5)

- Paraphrase:

But God, who created man for fellowship with Him, also created a plan whereby we can be united with Him. He sent His Son to die in our place, and through Christ's death, averted His wrath toward us. Therefore, we have fellowship with God.

For Christ also died for sins once for all, the just for the unjust, in order that He might bring us to God... (1 Pet. 3:18)

- Paraphrase:

For the grace of God has appeared, bringing salvation to all men,
instructing us to deny ungodliness and worldly desires and to live sensibly, righteously and godly in the present age,

40

looking for the blessed hope and the appearing of the glory of our great God and Savior, Christ Jesus;
who gave Himself for us, that He might redeem us from every lawless deed and purify for Himself a people for His own possession, zealous for good deeds. (Titus 2:11-14)

- Paraphrase:

And there is salvation in no one else; for there is no other name under heaven that has been given among men, by which we must be saved. (Acts 4:12)

- Paraphrase:

- From your paraphrases above, write a summary statement about the Lord's purpose:

Unconditional love

Sacrificing His only Son's life on our behalf is overwhelming evidence of God's love for us.

By this the love of God was manifested in us, that God has sent His only begotten Son into the world so that we might live through Him.
In this is love, not that we loved God, but that He loved us and sent His Son to be the propitiation for our sins. (1 John 4:9-10)

- Paraphrase:

For God so loved the world, that He gave His only begotten Son, that whoever believes in Him should not perish, but have eternal life. For God did not send the Son into the world to judge the world, but that the world should be saved through Him. He who believes in Him is not judged; he who does not believe has been judged already, because he has not believed in the name of the only begotten Son of God. (John 3:16-18)

- Paraphrase:

- From your paraphrases above, write a summary statement about God's unconditional love:

Complete forgiveness

Christ's death not only averted the wrath of God from those who believe in Him, but completely paid our debt of sin so that we are completely forgiven.

And when you were dead in your transgressions and the uncircumcision of your flesh, He made you alive together with Him, having forgiven us all our transgressions,
having canceled out the certificate of debt consisting of decrees against us and which was hostile to us; and He has taken it out of the way, having nailed it to the cross. (Col. 2:13-14)

- Paraphrase:

For while we were still helpless, at the right time Christ died for the ungodly.
For one will hardly die for a righteous man; though perhaps for the good man someone would dare even to die.
But God demonstrates His own love toward us, in that while we were yet sinners, Christ died for us.
Much more then, having now been justified by His blood, we shall be saved from the wrath of God through Him.
For if while we were enemies, we were reconciled to God through the death of His Son, much more, having been reconciled, we shall be saved by His life.
And not only this, but we also exult in God through our Lord Jesus Christ, through whom we have now received the reconciliation. (Rom. 5:6-11)

- Paraphrase:

Because we are forgiven by God, we can forgive others.

...bearing with one another, and forgiving each other, whoever has a complaint against anyone; just as the Lord forgave you, so also should you. (Col. 3:13)

- Paraphrase:

Now one of the Pharisees was requesting Him to dine with him. And He entered the Pharisee's house, and reclined at the table.
And behold, there was a woman in the city who was a sinner; and when she learned that He was reclining at the table in the Pharisee's house, she brought an alabaster vial of perfume,

and standing behind Him at His feet, weeping, she began to wet His feet with her tears, and kept wiping them with the hair of her head, and kissing His feet, and anointing them with the perfume.

Now when the Pharisee who had invited Him saw this, he said to himself, "If this man were a prophet He would know who and what sort of person this woman is who is touching Him, that she is a sinner."

And Jesus answered and said to him, "Simon, I have something to say to you." And he replied, "Say it, Teacher."

"A certain moneylender had two debtors; one owed five hundred denarii, and the other fifty.

When they were unable to repay, he graciously forgave them both. Which of them therefore will love him more?"

Simon answered and said, "I suppose the one whom he forgave more." And He said to him, "You have judged correctly."

And turning toward the woman, He said to Simon, "Do you see this woman? I entered your house; you gave Me no water for My feet, but she has wet My feet with her tears, and wiped them with her hair.

You gave Me no kiss; but she, since the time I came in, has not ceased to kiss My feet. You did not anoint My head with oil, but she anointed My feet with perfume.

For this reason I say to you, her sins, which are many, have been forgiven, for she loved much; but he who is forgiven little loves little."

And He said to her, "Your sins have been forgive." (Luke 7:36-48)

- Paraphrase:

- From your paraphrases above, write a summary statement about the Lord's complete forgiveness:

Total acceptance

Christ's payment for our sins took away the barrier between Him and us so that we are now His beloved children and His beloved friends.

For you have not received a spirit of slavery leading to fear again, but you have received a spirit of adoption as sons by which we cry out, "Abba! Father!"
The Spirit Himself bears witness with our spirit that we are children of God,
and if children, heirs also, heirs of God and fellow heirs with Christ, if indeed we suffer with Him in order that we may also be glorified with Him. (Rom. 8:15-17)

- Paraphrase:

...in order that He might redeem those who were under the Law, that we might receive the adoption as sons.

And because you are sons, God has sent forth the Spirit of His Son into our hearts, crying, "Abba! Father!"

Therefore you are no longer a slave, but a son; and if a son, then an heir through God. (Gal. 4:5-7)

- Paraphrase:

Because we are totally accepted by God, we can unconditionally accept others.

Wherefore, accept one another, just as Christ also accepted us to the glory of God. (Rom. 15:7)

- Paraphrase:

- Write a summary statement about God's total acceptance of us:

Authority and power

Christ has infinite authority and power. In His life and death on earth, He achieved our redemption. He defeated every temptation known to man (Heb. 2:14-15; 4:15), reconciled us to God (Matt. 26:28; Rom. 5:8), and triumphed over every evil power and authority (Col. 2:15). His resurrection proves that He has authority over death and that He is alive today (Luke 24:1-49; 1 Cor. 15:3-4), and His ascension sealed His victory and ours (Mark 16:19; Luke 24:50-53; Acts 1:1-11). Scripture tells us that Jesus Christ is now seated at the right hand of God *in the heavenly places, far above all rule and authority and power and dominion, and every name that is named, not only in this age, but also in the one to come,* and that all things are in subjection to Him (Eph. 1:20-22).

Paraphrase the following passages about Christ's authority and power:

44

When He had disarmed the rulers and authorities, He made a public display of them, having triumphed over them through Him. (Col. 2:15)

- Paraphrase:

And He is the image of the invisible God, the first-born of all creation.
For by Him all things were created, both in the heavens and on earth, visible and invisible, whether thrones or dominions or rulers or authorities – all things have been created by Him and for Him.
And He is before all things, and in Him all things hold together.
He is also the head of the body, the church; and He is the beginning, the first-born from the dead; so that He Himself might come to have first place in everything.
For it was the Father's good pleasure for all the fullness to dwell in Him, and through Him to reconcile all things to Himself, having made peace through the blood of His cross; through Him, I say, whether things on earth or things in heaven. (Col. 1:15-19)

- Paraphrase:

... and in Him you have been made complete, and He is the head over all rule and authority... (Col. 2:10)

- Paraphrase:

Therefore also God highly exalted Him, and bestowed on Him the name which is above every name,
that at the name of Jesus every knee should bow, of those who are in heaven, and on earth, and under the earth,
and that every tongue should confess that Jesus Christ is Lord, to the glory of God the Father. (Phil. 2:9-11)

- Paraphrase:

- Write a summary statement about the Lord's authority and power:

Hope
There is no hope of forgiveness and reconciliation to God apart from Christ.

...remember that you were at that time separate from Christ, excluded from the commonwealth of Israel, and strangers to the covenants of promise, having no hope and without God in the world. (Eph. 2:12)

- Paraphrase:

But His love, forgiveness, and power give us hope for a new life.

Blessed be the God and Father of our Lord Jesus Christ, who according to His great mercy has caused us to be born again to a living hope through the resurrection of Jesus Christ from the dead...(1 Pet. 1:3)

- Paraphrase:

And we know that God causes all things to work together for good to those who love God, to those who are called according to His purpose. (Rom. 8:28)

- Paraphrase:

- Write a summary statement about the hope of Christ:

Faithfulness

Christ is always faithful to do what He has promised.

No temptation has overtaken you but such as is common to man; and God is faithful, who will not allow you to be tempted beyond what you are able, but with the temptation will provide the way of escape also, that you may be able to endure it. (1 Cor. 10:13)

- Paraphrase:

Let us hold fast the confession of our hope without wavering; for He who promised is faithful... (Heb. 10:23)

- Paraphrase:

It is a trustworthy statement: For if we died with Him, we shall also live with Him; If we endure, we shall also reign with Him; if we deny Him, He also will deny us; If we are faithless, He remains faithful; for He cannot deny Himself. (2 Tim. 2:11-13)

- Paraphrase:

- Write a summary statement about the Lord's faithfulness:

Wisdom

The Lord has all knowledge and all wisdom. He knows what is best for us, and He will give us wisdom to know how we can honor Him in every situation.

But if any of you lacks wisdom, let him ask of God, who gives to all men generously and without reproach, and it will be given to him.
But let him ask in faith without any doubting, for the one who doubts is like the surf of the sea driven and tossed by the wind. (James 1:5-6)

- Paraphrase:

For the word of the cross is to those who are perishing foolishness, but to us who are being saved it is the power of God.
For it is written, "I will destroy the wisdom of the wise, and the cleverness of the clever I will set aside."
Where is the wise man? Where is the scribe: Where is the debater of this age: Has not God made foolish the wisdom of the world?
For since in the wisdom of God the world through its wisdom did not come to know God, God was well-pleased through the foolishness of the message preached to save those who believe.
For indeed Jews ask for signs and Greeks search for wisdom; but we preach Christ crucified, to Jews a stumbling block, and to Gentiles foolishness,
but to those who are the called, both Jews and Greeks, Christ the power of God and the wisdom of God.
Because the foolishness of God is wiser than men, and the weakness of God is stronger than men.
For consider your calling, brethren, that there were not many wise according to the flesh, not many mighty, not many noble;
but God has chosen the foolish things of the world to shame the wise, and God has chosen the weak things of the world to shame the things which are strong ...
(1 Cor. 1:18-27)

- Paraphrase:

"For My thoughts are not your thoughts, neither are your ways My ways," declares the Lord.
"For as the heavens are higher than the earth, so are My ways higher than your ways, and My thoughts than your thoughts." (Is. 55:8-9)
Paraphrase:

Therefore be careful how you walk, not as unwise men, but as wise,
making the most of your time, because the days are evil.
So then do not be foolish, but understand what the will of the Lord is.

And do not get drunk with wine, for that is dissipation, but be filled with the Spirit, speaking to one another in psalms and hymns and spiritual songs, singing and making melody with your heart to the Lord;

always giving thanks for all things in the name of our Lord Jesus Christ to God, even the Father;

and be subject to one another in the fear of Christ. (Eph. 5:15-21)

- Paraphrase:

- Write a summary statement about the Lord's wisdom:

Trusting in Christ

Augustine observed, "Thou hast made us for Thyself, O God, and the heart of man is restless until it finds its rest in Thee." God desires to have an intimate relationship with us, and He has given us a provision for continual access to him through His Son, Jesus Christ (John 3:16-17; Heb. 2:17). John 1:12 says, *But as many as received Him, to them He gave the right to become children of God, even to those who believe in His name.*

Are you trusting in your own abilities to earn acceptance with God, or are you trusting in the death of Christ to pay for your sins, and the resurrection of Christ to give you new life? Take a moment to reflect on this question: *On a scale of 0-100 percent, how sure are you that you would spend eternity with God if you died today?* An answer of less than 100 percent may indicate that you are trusting, at least in part, in yourself. You may be thinking, *Isn't it arrogant to say that I am 100 percent sure?* Indeed, it would be arrogance if you were trusting in yourself – your abilities, your actions and good deeds – to earn your salvation. However, if you are no longer trusting in your own efforts, but in the all-sufficient payment of Christ, then 100 percent certainty is a response of humility and thankfulness, nor arrogance.

Reflect on a second question: *If you were to die today and stand before God, and He were to ask you, "Why should I let you into heaven?" what would you tell Him?* Would you mention your abilities, church attendance, kindness to others, Christian service, abstinence from a particular sin, or some other good deed? Paul wrote to Titus:

But when the kindness of God our Savior and His love for mankind appeared,
He saved us, not on the basis of deeds which we have done in righteousness, but according to His mercy...(Titus 3:4-5)

And to the Ephesians he wrote:
For by grace you have been saved through faith; and that not of yourselves, it is the gift of God;
not as a result of works, that no one should boast. (Eph. 2:8-9)

We must give up our own efforts to achieve righteousness, and instead believe that Christ's death and resurrection alone are sufficient to pay for our sin and separation from God.

In Acts 16:31, Luke wrote,... *Believe in the Lord Jesus, and you shall be saved...* Jesus said: *I am the way, and the truth, and the life; no one comes to the Father, but through Me* (John 14:6).

We receive Jesus by invitation. He does not force Himself on us, but says:

Behold I stand at the door and knock; if anyone hears My voice and opens the door, I will come in to him, and will dine with him, and he with Me. (Rev. 3:20)

Take some time to reflect on the two questions we examined earlier. Reflect on God's love, which He has expressed to you by sending His only Son to die in your place. Read Luke 22:39-46. Consider the selfless sacrifice of Jesus to carry out this divine plan. Realize that if you were the only person to walk this earth, Jesus would have done this for *you*.

If you are not 100 percent sure that you would spend eternity with God if you died today, and if you are willing to trust in Christ and accept His payment for your sins, you may use this prayer to express your faith:

Lord Jesus, I need You. I want You to be my Savior and my Lord. I accept Your death on the cross as payment for my sins, and now entrust my life to Your care. Thank You for forgiving me and for giving me a new life. Thank You for the new life that is now mine through You. Please help me grow in my understanding of Your love and power so that my life will bring glory and honor to You. Amen.

(date)	(signature)

If you have placed your trust in Jesus Christ prior to reading this, consider reaffirming your faith and commitment to serve Him. You may do so by using this prayer:

Lord, Jesus, I need You, and thank You that I am Yours. I confess that I have sinned against You, and ask You to "create in me a clean heart, and renew a steadfast spirit within me" (Ps 51:10). I renew my commitment to serve You. Thank You for loving me and for forgiving me. Please give me Your strength and wisdom to continue growing in You so that my life can bring glory and honor to You. Amen.

(date)	(signature)

It is important to understand that trusting in Christ does not guarantee an instantaneous deliverance from compulsive behavior or any other problem in life. However, it does mean that you are forgiven for your rebellion against God; that you are restored to a relationship with Him that will last throughout eternity; and that you will receive His unconditional love and acceptance, as well as His strength and wisdom, as you continue to grow in recovery.

Baptism

Some people may ask, "How does baptism relate to one's conversion experience?" Water baptism is an outward demonstration of a believer's internal commitment to Christ. It enables the believer to identify himself with Christ in his culture. The act of baptism symbolizes his being dead, buried, and raised with Christ. In the early church and in some countries today, this identification, is a dramatic statement of being severed from the world and being bonded to the body of Christ. In our society, it is still an important step of obedience as we identify ourselves publicly with Christ and His people. (For a sample of passages on Spirit or water baptism, see Acts 8:26-39; Rom. 6:1-4; and 1 Cor. 12:13.)

As a result of our trust in Christ, there are many facts and promises in God's Word that we can depend on. Facts are truths that are *already* true of us; *promises* are statements that we know will be fulfilled because of the trustworthiness of God. Here is a very short list of both:

Facts from God's Word

You are completely forgiven by God (Rom. 3:19-25; Col. 2:13-14).
You are righteous and pleasing to God (2 Cor. 5:21).
You are totally accepted by God (Col. 1:19-22).
You are deeply loved by God (1 John 4:9-10).
You are absolutely complete in Christ (2 Cor. 5:17; Col. 2:10).
The Holy Spirit dwells in you (Rom. 8:9-11).
You are God's child (Rom. 8:15-16)
You are a fellow heir with Christ (Rom. 8:17).
God works all things for good for those who love Him (Rom. 8:28).

Promises from God's Word

Christ will never leave us (Matt. 28:20; Heb. 13:5).
He will abundantly provide for our needs (Phil. 4:10).
We will be in heaven with Him (John 14:1-3).
We will reign with Him (2 Tim. 2:12).
He will strengthen us (Is. 40:29).
He will give us His peace (John 14:27).
He will accomplish His purposes (1 Thess. 5:24).
He will enable us to give generously (2 Cor. 9:6-11).
We will be persecuted (John 15:18-21)

STEP FOUR

We make a searching and fearless moral inventory of ourselves.

Let us examine and probe our ways, and let us return to the Lord. (Lam. 3:40)

We have learned from step 2, that *sanity* can mean exercising sound judgment or making wise, rational decisions. In step 4, we will see that the best way to determine the course of our future path – using sound judgment – is to obtain the facts about our past. No merchant runs a successful business without taking inventory. A thorough overview of his business tells him what products to eliminate, what to order more of, and what new products to try. An inventory of ourselves will accomplish much the same purpose. Reviewing our past enables us to work today toward a successful tomorrow.

In step 4, we will examine what we've done well and what we've done poorly. Perhaps we have made improvements in an area of life that has always been difficult for us. We may have taken some action – however large or small – to promote love, kindness, consideration, healing, or health. However, in order to take a thorough inventory, we must also ask what we've done – to ourselves and others – to cause pain, bitterness, fear, or separation. Have we allowed anger and resentment to dominate our relationships? Have we been manipulative of other people, selfish, dishonest, or disloyal? How have we handled our sexuality? Step 4 will help us to determine what characteristics and actions we need to eliminate from our "inventory" and what we can begin to substitute in their place.

Just as importantly, an appraisal of our past behavior gives us an opportunity to confess sins we may not yet be aware of. This releases us from the bondage of destructive guilt, reconciles us to God, and frees us for future service to him. Proverbs 28:13 says, *He who conceals his transgressions will not prosper, but he who confesses and forsakes them will find compassion.*

A review of our past often gives us an understanding of *why* we behaved in certain ways at certain times. By becoming more aware of destructive patterns in our behavior, we are better able to make appropriate responses to similar situations in the future. Also, by understanding the why's of our behavior, we often gain a new acceptance of ourselves. A positive sense of self-respect begins to emerge, and with it, a new tolerance for other people.

Finally, an objective review of the past enables us to confront our age-old enemy: denial. In the past, denial seemed to work well for us. With it, we could escape from hurtful remarks, a deteriorating self-image, frightful responsibilities, and worrisome circumstances.

In reality, denial was just a defense mechanism which prevented us from progressing in our lives. It was an ineffective way to cope with adult behavior and responsibilities.

As our denial begins to crumble, we will begin to see the truth about our lives. We will see that our addictive behavior caused problems in our relationships, that we had trouble controlling our emotions, that we were desperately unhappy – often filled with fear, a sense of isolation, uselessness, and self-pity.

We used alcohol or drugs to fill our emptiness. We worked hard to control circumstances and loved ones to get our needs met. Increasingly unable to tolerate ourselves, we projected our self-hatred onto other people. We may have been physically or verbally abusive. Or, we may have repressed our negative emotions and nursed our grudges and resentments, believing we had a "right" to such feelings.

While the drinking or drug abuse may have since stopped, these problems cannot be resolved unaided. They must be confessed, drawn out into God's light and love, and released – the purpose of step 4.

"The Past" is a frightening prospect for many of us. When confronted with it, we are apt to consider that sin or those sins we'd hoped to carry to our grave. But hiding sins is detrimental to our welfare (and will, in fact, send the chemically dependent person back to drink or drugs).

Step 4 is not intended to increase your sense of shame and guilt, but is instead designed to bring the hidden areas of your life into God's light so that you might experience His grace more fully (1 John 1:5-10).

The Lord *is* gracious. According to Heb. 4:15-16,...*we do not have a high priest who cannot sympathize with our weaknesses, but one who has been tempted in all things as we are, yet without sin. Let us therefore draw near with confidence to the throne of grace, that we may receive mercy and may find grace to help in time of need.*

Help and mercy are ours for the asking; we can therefore be fearless as we approach this step, knowing that our Lord will not reveal to us more than we can handle at any given time. He knows us; we can be completely honest with Him and with ourselves as we examine both our faults and our strengths.

Take your time in completing this inventory. Try to work through one characteristic per day. Your only goal in this exercise is to think, reflect, and examine your life. Ask God to show you what He wants you to see about your past, and then trust him to reveal to you *what* you need to know *when* need to know it.

Resentment

Webster's Ninth Collegiate Dictionary defines *resentment* as " a feeling of indignant displeasure or persistent ill will at something regarded as a wrong, insult, or injury."

Resentment often grows from the seed of unmet expectations – in our experience with God, with organizations, situations, and with other people. A loved one is struck with terminal illness, and we shake our fist at God. We work hard for a living and are laid off in tough economic times. We share a confidence with someone we trust and are abandoned or betrayed. Our spouse has an affair and we cannot forgive.

The feeling of resentment is not wrong; however, if prolonged, resentment can lead to bitterness. Hebrews 12:15 says, *See to it that no one misses the grace of God and that no bitter root grows up to cause trouble and defile many* (NIV).

Resentment causes us to miss the grace of God in our relationships and circumstances because we are more absorbed with our "rights" than with the love and forgiveness He has extended to us. In the end, we are the big loser. Resentment can result in physical illnesses, stifled creativity, ruined relationships, and doubt in our relationship with God due to our inability to accept His love.

List some ways that people have expressed resentment toward you:

Describe some ways that you have expressed resentment toward others:

What usually causes you to feel resentful?

Paraphrase Matt. 18:21-35.

- What does this passage teach about withholding forgiveness from others?

Forgiveness

Forgiveness means giving up the desire to punish the one who has offended us. One author has written that three elements are essential to the process of forgiving: and injury, a debt resulting from the injury, and a cancellation of the debt.[1] However, rather than recognize an injury and count the cost we've incurred as a result of it, many of us tend to minimize (or even negate) its value and excuse the offender: *She couldn't help it,* we often tell ourselves, or, *He didn't really mean to hurt me.* Responses like these may sound noble, but they obstruct honesty, and consequently, block our ability to extend complete forgiveness.

Discounting the magnitude of both our sin and Christ's payment for it on the cross also contributes to our inability to forgive others (Luke 7:36-50). In addition, many of us are convinced that we have to earn forgiveness from God. We may therefore punish those who offend us in an attempt to ensure that they "pay for " their sins against us.

Again, forgiveness is an informed decision to bear the pain of another's offense without demanding that he or she be punished for it. This does not mean that we are to overlook or accept unacceptable behavior, nor should we allow the offender to continue in his or her wrongful behavior toward us. Rather, the process of forgiving may include exercising "tough love." This may mean talking with the person who has hurt us about his or her behavior and/or allowing him or her to experience any negative consequences

53

resulting from that behavior. This enables the offender to understand at least some of the effects of his or her wrongdoing. Such an experience may or may not prompt change in the offender's behavior, and may or may not be the basis of change in our relationship with him or her. However, regardless of another person's response, we still are responsible for forgiving anyone who offends us.

Why should we forgive?

God commands us to forgive others through Jesus Christ. "And whenever you stand praying, forgive, if you have anything against anyone…(Mark 11:25).

We have been forgiven by God through Jesus Christ. "And be kind to one another, tenderhearted, forgiving each other, just as God in Christ also has forgiven you" (Eph. 4:32).

An unforgiving spirit hurts us. Not forgiving often leads to suppressed hurts and anger. Repressing negative emotions affects our every relationship and leads to bitterness, depression, and alienation. This deadly combination can turn the dependent person back to drinking or using.

From step 3, describe the forgiveness you have in Christ. Explain what it is, how it was given, and how this affects you.

- Define *forgiveness:*

- How has God extended forgiveness to you through Christ?

- How does this affect you?

? Write what persons have offended you or harmed you. What did they do to you?

Example:

Person	Offense

What would it mean to release each person from the penalty he or she owes you?

Example:

Person	Result of Forgiveness

54

Have you forgiven any of them already? If so, explain how:

Example:

Person	Forgiveness

What have been the results of extending forgiveness…
- For you?
- For the offender(s)?

How can you tell that you've forgiven someone?

What are some of the emotional, relational, spiritual, and mental consequences of unforgivingness…
- For you?
- For the offender(s)?

Paraphrase Col. 3:13:

Dishonesty

   Dishonesty is a tremendous threat to sobriety. It damages our self-esteem. It hurts our relationship with God, who desires *truth in the innermost being* (Ps. 51:6), and it hurts our relationships with others. Dishonesty, we can be sure, will keep us in bondage to our addiction.

   Sarah had been anxious about problems within her family when she visited her physician for a routine exam. He prescribed tranquilizers to help her sleep, intending that she take one per day at bedtime. Sarah followed his instructions for about six months, but her anxiety persisted. Having discovered that a tranquilizer was soothing to her every time she became irritable, she began to increase her dosage. Later, she discovered that the drug's tranquil effect was even more pronounced when taken with a glass of wine. Within the course of ten years, Sarah developed a serious addiction to alcohol and drugs.

   In and effort to feed her addiction, Sarah conned her parents into "loaning" her money she never returned. She took money from her husband's wallet, and when asked about it, blamed the children. When her family finally made an attempt at intervention, Sarah employed guilt to convince them that they were the source of her troubles, and that they –

not she – needed help. She continued to use - and began hiding her prescription bottles. It wasn't until she was arrested for forging her physician's name at a pharmacy that Sarah "awakened" to the truth of her addiction and subsequent dishonesty.

Dishonesty manifests itself in many ways; among them:

- **Alibis:** Dishonesty attempts to justify improper behavior by making up excuses which are usually only partially true, or which are purely fiction.

- **Denial:** Denial may be manifested by an outright lie: "I didn't do it," said the man who was guilty of fraud. Or, it may be a refusal to believe or accept the truth about one's self, one's circumstances, or someone else. A classic case of denial is often demonstrated by the person who is addicted to alcohol or drugs, but is either unwilling or unable to admit to himself or anyone else.

- **Displaced Blame:** Dishonesty attempts to escape responsibility for a wrong by accusing someone else, or by blaming circumstances rather than accepting responsibility for wrongful behavior.

- **Exaggeration:** "Stretching" the truth to make things seem a little better or a little worse than they really are, often to impress someone else, or to cause others to take pity on us.

- **Minimizing:** Understanding the truth, often with the intent of making an offense seem smaller than it really is. For example, a person who has completely dented another person's car door in an accident may try to maintain that the damage is "only a scratch."

- **Stealing:** This seems obvious, but is it? Stealing comes in many subtle forms: taking work supplies home; "borrowing" money we never repay; using the company's Xerox machine for personal copies; stealing time at work by conducting personal business during office hours.

- **Lying:** Falsifying the truth would again seem obvious, but it often isn't. Many of us live in pretense with other people, flattering them and pretending to care for them when we really want something from them. Or, instead of telling others what we want, we condemn them and make them feel guilty, so that we can control and manipulate them. There are other forms of pretense, such as saying "We'll see," when we mean no; or, "I'd love to have you come," when we'd rather he or she not. We say we *must* do something when the truth is that we *want* to do something. The list is endless. The bottom line is that dishonesty has no place in sobriety.

Have you been dishonest in any of the following ways? If so, how? When? Why? Explain.

- Denial:

- Alibis:

- Displaced Blame:

- Exaggeration:

- Minimizing:

- Stealing:

- Lying:

Honesty

When we were bound to our compulsion, our egos – already frail – couldn't stand up to the truth about ourselves. We were too afraid of what we might see if we looked honestly at our behavior. But now that we're making improvements in our lives, we can afford to give ourselves an honest evaluation. We begin by taking this inventory.

Being truthful is easier now because there's less to hide. We no longer have to hide bottles, pills, or our compulsive addiction from others. Because we no longer have hangovers, we no longer have to pretend that we feel great like we did before when we were feeling lousy.

And, whether we are involved in a support group or in treatment, we are discovering that many others have faced, or are facing, some of the same problems we have experienced. While we find it wise to be discerning about what we say, knowing that there are others like us makes it easier to be genuine.

We also are now beginning to realize that we can always be honest with God. He made us. He knows our every thought, our every word, our every action. And He loves us anyway. His love for us is unconditional. What a relief to have One with whom we can be *totally* honest!

Name some areas in your life in which you now feel free to be honest:

What factors and people encourage you to be more honest about your life?

Has recovery been a source of help to you in becoming more honest? If so, explain:
In what aspects of your life have you had the most difficulty in being honest, and why?
How does being honest affect your self-esteem?

Paraphrase PS. 139:1-6:

57

Does realizing that the Lord already knows everything about you – both good and bad – help you to be more honest? Why, or why not?

Selfishness

With what are usually profound feeling of emptiness, chemically dependent persons often exhibit excessively compulsive behaviors. Acting compulsively is an attempt to meet legitimate needs in illegitimate ways. This was perpetuated by our addiction. We were driven by our desire to get "high" whenever we wanted, and were compelled by the fear that we would not have enough supply on hand to do so when the urge took over. Many of us began to hoard alcohol and/or drugs. Fueled by the drive for immediate gratification, we were always preoccupied with ourselves.

Such selfishness carried over into other affairs of life: sex, possessions, money, our social and professional status. Selfishness lay behind our acts of greed, jealousy, manipulation, protective denial, and angry revenge.

Ironically, the harder we worked toward self-satisfaction, the less satisfied we became.

Paraphrase Luke 12:15-21:

Why was the rich man in Luke described as a "fool"?

Different areas of selfishness are listed below. Identify those in which you have been selfish, and explain what you have hoped to gain, how you have treated others in the process, and how this has affected your relationships and self-esteem:

- money or possessions
- prestige, status
- sex
- attention

Describe some ways you've been selfish with **money or possessions:**

- What have you hoped to gain?
- How have you treated others in your pursuit of money or possessions?

- How has this affected your relationships?

- How has this affected your self-esteem?

58

Describe some ways you've been selfish in trying to achieve **prestige:**

- What have you hoped to gain?

- How have you treated others in this pursuit?

- How has this affected your relationships?

- How has this affected your self-esteem?

How have you been selfish in your pursuit of **sex**?

- What have you hoped to gain?

- How have you treated others in your pursuit of sex?

- How has this affected your relationships?

- How has this affected your self-esteem?

How have you been selfish in your pursuit of **attention?**

- What have you hoped to gain?

- How have you treated others in the process?

- How has this affected your relationships?

- How has this affected your self-esteem?

- What have you just learned? Write a concluding statement:

Gratitude

As our mental, emotional, physical, and spiritual well-being is gradually restored, we are becoming more thankful, realizing that the changes we and other people are beginning to see within us are the gift of God through Christ.

Our gratitude motivates us to share this news with other people. Also, because we are starting to feel better about ourselves, and are less preoccupied with our well-being, we begin wanting to share our resources with other people: our time, energies, talents, and sometimes, even our finances.

Some of us may be surprised to discover that giving of ourselves brings us great satisfaction. ...*freely you received, freely give (*Matt. 10:8).

Complete the following statement: *Contentment comes...*

Make a list of the people, situations, and things for which you are thankful:

What do you have that you can share with someone else?

What are you already sharing with others?

How are you sharing...

- Your resources?

- Your possessions?

- Yourself?

Impatience and Impulsiveness

I want what I want – now! Impatience may have been characteristic of our lives prior to addiction, but certainly it was rampant during our addiction. We gulped drinks and/or pills for immediate satisfaction. We exploited our senses to feel good fast. This trait, like all the others, carried over into our relationships. We barked out orders, and by our actions and attitudes, demanded that those around us "shape up" and "get in line" *now*. We were impatient at work, always hurrying to meet deadlines, hoping to prove ourselves and move to the top. We were thus quite often annoyed with coworkers who placed demands on our time, or who presented us with obstacles that might impede our immediate success. Impatience carried over into our social lives. Many of us spent money we didn't have, wanting to impress others with overnight success stories.

Looking back, we realize that impatience robbed us of a number of the joys in life. For many of us, the "tyranny of the urgent" eventually compounded our physical problems, caused us to rely more heavily on chemical substances, and nearly destroyed our relationships with those most important to us.

In what ways are you impatient or impulsive?

What is your understanding of your need for immediacy?

What people and circumstances seem to provoke feelings of impatience within you?

Example:

People	Circumstances

Using the list made in the above response, what do you usually say and do at these times?

Example:

People	Response

Name some consequences of impatience and impulsiveness in...

- Your life:

- Your relationships:

- How has the above affected your self-esteem?

Paraphrase Eph. 4:1-3:

Patience

Recovery provides an opportunity for us to learn patience. Gone is the immediate escape and gratification once provided by alcohol and/or drugs. Gone for many of us is the sense of security experienced when others were acting as our rescuers and caretakers. The result is that we are gradually recognizing our limitations, and are beginning to slow down a little. In so doing, we are exercising patience.

In recovery, we demonstrate patience each time we outlast an urge to drink or use. We exercise patience when we begin to control our spending and other habits. We develop patience as we look for God's will and wait for His direction. Patience allows us to receive more enjoyment from others. And to give more enjoyment to them.

Patience is a form of self-control, and self-control is a demonstration of the Holy Spirit's work within us (Gal. 5:22-23).

How might God's grace, love, forgiveness, and acceptance help you overcome impatience?

How are you applying (or how can you apply) these characteristics of God to yourself and to others in the circumstances you listed in your Impatience Inventory?

Name some possible results in your life and relationships as you learn to be patient through experiencing God's love, forgiveness, and acceptance:

From Phil. 4:5-7, how can the Lord help you to be more peaceful and patient?

False Pride/False Humility

Among the many ailments ascribed to chemical dependency, false pride and false humility are among the most detrimental. These are black-or-white perspectives in which one oscillates between being the "Great I Am" and the "Poor Me."

False pride obstructs recovery because it is based on the notion that we don't need the help of God or other people, thank you; we are self-sufficient. Those who manifest this trait to do so by an unwillingness to be wrong and apologize; by an unwillingness to admit powerlessness over any habit, including chemical dependency.

False humility is self-devaluation. It blocks recovery because it is founded on negative conclusions from past experiences rather than on an accurate appraisal of our self-worth in God's eyes. False humility is often characterized by self-condemnation, passivity, fear, a sense of hopelessness and defeat.

The Apostle Paul wrote the Romans: ...*I say to every man among you not to think more highly of himself than he ought to think; but to think so as to have sound judgment, as God has allotted to each a measure of faith* (Rom. 12:3).

On what occasions have you thought of yourself as the "Great I Am"?

• Why do you think you've felt this way about yourself from time to time?

• How has false pride hurt you and your relationships?

In what situations have you experienced fear, a sense of hopelessness, or defeat?

- Why do you think you've felt this way?

- How have these feelings affected you and your relationships?

Paraphrase Rom. 12:3:

In what kinds of situations do you tend to act passively, and why?

Humility

Our humility began with the acknowledgment that we are powerless over chemical substances. It continues to take a place within our lives as we daily submit ourselves to God for continued restoration.

Having received His beneficial help during these initial stages of recovery, we have realized the need we have for support from other people. When we are feeling out of sorts or tempted to indulge our addiction, we call on others or attend a support meeting. The fellowship we find there helps to meet the needs we once tried to fill with chemical substances.

By listening to other people who share our predicament, we realize that everyone has strengths and weaknesses – including us. And we realize that it is okay to be human, to be genuine with other people and with God.

Paraphrase Phil. 2:3-4:

Define *humility* in your own words:

Are you practicing humility: If so, how?

Is humility a sign of weakness? Why, or why not?

Does the idea of being humble frighten and/or disgust you? If so, how?

Name some ways humility can be a sign of objectivity and strength:

How would (or how does) practicing humility affect your life, your relationship with God, and your relationships with other people?

- Your life:

- Your relationship with God:

- Your relationships with other people:

Destructive Anger

Anger is a God-given emotional response that we all experience on occasion. Surrendered to God and used wisely, with control, it can have a positive result. Unaided and unimpeded, however, anger can have tragic consequences.

Anger can be a response to unmet expectations; irritation or frustration when things don't go our way; or a demonstration of hostility when someone has a different opinion. Anger can also be a defensive response to a hurtful attack or to be a real or perceived threat to one's self-esteem or well-being.

Like anything else, it is okay to *feel* angry. What we do with it is something else. Many of us use our anger destructively rather that constructively.

Destructive anger can be expressed outwardly or inwardly; either way, it can result in depression, suspicion, and a low sense of self-worth. Examples of destructive anger are verbal abuse (screaming, criticism, fault-finding), physical abuse, teasing, sarcasm, and murder. Silence, neglect, and withdrawal can also be destructive expressions of anger.

The Apostle Paul wrote: *Be angry, and yet do not sin; do not let the sun go down on your anger, and do not give the devil an opportunity* (Eph. 4:26-27).

Destructive anger can have catastrophic effects on our recovery. Expressed outwardly, it can alienate us from others and drive a wedge between God and us. Without these sources of help, the addicted person is likely to return to his habit to fill the void of emptiness in his life. Anger turned inward is also dangerous. The dependent person has a low tolerance for the burdening effects of repressed anger. If anger is not dealt with constructively, he will usually return to his habit for relief from these negative emotions.

From the above, how do you usually express anger, and why?

- Are these primarily inward or outward expressions of anger?

Do particular people or situations seem to trigger your anger? If so, describe:
Cite three examples of how destructive anger has affected you and your relationships.

Example:

SITUATION:
Response:
Result:

Constructive Anger

In recovery, we begin to discover ways we can channel anger into positive action. Because we are releasing our grip on denial, we can more often admit feelings of anger, first to ourselves and then to God.

The biblical King David offers a good illustration of handling negative emotions like anger positively. After his anointing as king, and before his induction as ruler over Israel, David was continually assaulted by his outraged, half-crazed father-in-law, Saul, who was then the ruler over Israel, and who wanted to kill David. Under constant attack, David had every reason to be defensive and angry. Yet David was able to both honor Saul and to gain victory over his negative emotions because he had learned to express those emotions to God (see 1Sam. 26:1-25). Psalms 42 and 58 are two of many examples of this:

> I say to God my Rock, "Why have you forgotten me?
> Why must I go about mourning, oppressed by the enemy?"
> Ps. 42:9-10. NIV

> Break the teeth in their mouths, O God; tear out, O Lord, the fangs of the lions!
> Let them vanish like water that flows away; when they draw the bow, let their arrows be   blunted.
> Like a slug melting away as it moves along, like a stillborn child, may they not see the   sun.
> Before your pots can feel the heat of the thorns — whether they be green or dry – the   wicked will be swept away.
> Ps. 58:6-9, NIV

David used his anger constructively; it drove him to his knees. Once we can admit that we are angry, we can ask God for His direction in our response. We can call our sponsor or a friend who can add objectivity to our situation. Then, if necessary, we can confront the offender with an attitude of love.

Constructive anger can give us the momentum we need to detach from a manipulative person or a harmful situation. It can give us the incentive to confront someone in love; it can motivate us to stop drinking or using.

As we progress in recovery, we gradually learn that anger is a gift from God, intended to compel us to provide loving correction and to confront the evils which threaten His purposes. We can only begin to do this as He intends by seeking His direction before we make our response.

List some differences between constructive and destructive anger:

Example:

Constructive Anger	Destructive Anger

What are some examples of using anger constructively?

Have you been able to use your anger constructively? If so, describe three situations with the results of having done this in each.

Example:

SITUATION:
Response:
Result:

Fear

Fear is a God-given emotional response to the awareness of danger. In proper perspective and in certain situations, it has an appropriate place in all of our lives. Fear can prompt us to make decisions necessary for survival. We exercise fear wisely when we warn children to avoid playing with matches, to stay away from strangers, and to look both ways when crossing the street. A constructive response to fear includes taking precautions against disease, theft, and natural disasters.

When we were drinking or using, however, fear usually played a dictatorial role in our lives, and our response to it was more often destructive than constructive.

Fear blocked our ability to love; we limited our social involvement. Fear motivated us to avoid risks of failure and rejection; we abused our bodies with chemicals for comfort and security. Fear relegated us to a need to be in control; we often mistreated and manipulated others to get our way. Fear prompted us to schedule our lives around our next fix; we hid bottles and/or drugs around the house to avoid withdrawal.

Now that we're not drinking or using, we may still experience a lot of fear. Feeling afraid is okay. But it need not consume us. Sobriety gives us an opportunity to learn how to examine fear objectively and utilize it constructively; to recognize it as a signal to correct something that's wrong within us or around us. It is helpful to talk with a trusted friend about our fears to see if they're reasonable. It is also wise to take them to God. He does not want us to be imprisoned by fear. *For God has not given us a spirit of timidity, but of power and love and discipline* (2 Tim. 1:7). *His perfect love casts out fear* (1 John 4:18).

Read Rom. 8:15. How are slavery and adoption contrasted?

What does each produce?

- Slavery:

- Adoption:

Whom or what do you fear most?

- Why?

How does fear control...

- Your attitudes?

- Your actions?

- Your relationships?

- Your sense of freedom?

Trust

In recovery, we develop the courage to acknowledge our fears and move forward with our lives in spite of them. As we do, we exercise trust and discover truth.

Many of our fears are actually rooted in lies. For example, many of us were convinced that we would meet with catastrophe if we couldn't drink or use. We were quite terrified of sobriety. Now we are learning that while we are challenged by the many facets of recovery, its benefits far outweigh the short-term gratification we once received from drinking or using. That's the truth. We had to exercise some faith to find it.

Faith was also required when we placed our trust in Jesus Christ. Now we are discovering that He can do a better job of directing our lives than we ever could have done. By developing trust in Him, we begin to learn that we can afford to take the risks of getting to know some people and trying some new things. Fellowship is helpful to our recovery. So is knowing that if we're rejected, He still accepts us, and if we fail, He still loves us.

Scripture tells us that trusting in God is the way to experience peace: *The steadfast of mind Thou wilt keep in perfect peace, because he trusts in Thee* (Is. 26:3).

Read Ps. 27:1-3, 13-14. Describe David's trust in the Lord:

Contrast the effects of fear and trust in a person's life:

Example:

Fear	Trust

How do we develop trust?

How has Christ shown Himself to be trustworthy?

What have you trusted Him to be or do for you?

Intolerance

Growing out of an increasing tolerance for chemical substances was a lack of tolerance for physical, mental, emotional, and relational conditions that were especially demanding.

For example, when we were living in addiction, we often neglected our bodies of proper nourishment. Rather than eating when hungry, we drank or used chemicals to satisfy our bodily needs.

Addiction led to emotional intolerance. Burdened by resentment, anger often prompted us to drink or use "at" someone or some circumstance. We may have been abusive – in our words and our actions.

During the course of our chemical abuse, we often may have demonstrated a lack of tolerance for people who had a different way of thinking of doing things. Not only this, but people usually had a way of getting between us and our habit. Intentionally or not, we isolated ourselves from others; then, lonely for companionship, we used or drank in an attempt to fill the emptiness within and meet our needs for intimacy.

The physical conditions of our lives also became unmanageable as hangovers and other symptoms of substance abuse drove us to exhaustion.

Our intolerance was the result of an inability to recognize our limitations.

How have you been demanding and intolerant toward…

- Your family?

- Yourself?

- Others?

- God?

How do emptiness and loneliness lend themselves to intolerance?

Tolerance

Now that we are recovering and have begun to assume responsibility for our physical, mental, spiritual, and emotional health, we will do well to remember the acronym: **HALT.** When compelled to use or drink, we must ask: *Am I*

> H ungry?
> A ngry?
> L onely?
> T ired?

These are warning signs. Unheeded, they can lead us back into drinking or drugging. We HALT to analyze our condition, and then HALT what we are doing to make an appropriate, healthy response.

In recovery, we also learn to demonstrate a healthy sense of tolerance for other *people*, even though we can't (and should not) always tolerate their *behavior*.

> *God grant me the serenity*
> *To accept the things I cannot change,*
> *Courage to change the things I can,*
> *And wisdom to know the difference.*
>   "The Serenity Prayer"

Read Eph. 4:17-24. How can you develop the habit of making good choices?

How can remembering to HALT help you to tolerate difficult people and circumstances?

What behaviors should you refuse to tolerate in yourself or others?

How are you demonstrating tolerance…

- Toward yourself?

- Toward others?

- In your circumstances?

Jealousy

Jealousy is born from ingratitude and bred by comparison. It is never satisfied. Usually, it does not have all the facts.

We envy someone else's circumstances because they *seem* to be better than ours. We imagine that our lives would be much improved if only we could acquire the position, talent, home, or spouse of a neighbor or friend.

Jealousy is characterized by the false notion that we *must* have something or someone to reach our potential and be happy. This compels us to focus on the things we lack and long for, rather than on the many blessings we've already received. By doing this, we miss many of the joys in life and set ourselves up for tremendous disappointment and unhappiness.

If not terminated, jealousy can lead to fits of rage and manifest itself in acts of violence. James 1:14-15 says: *But each one is tempted when he is carried away and enticed by his own lust. Then when lust has conceived, it gives birth to sin; and when sin is accomplished, it brings forth death.* One of the clearest examples of this found in the account of Christ's crucifixion when the chief priests and elders delivered Jesus to death *because of envy* (see Matt. 27:17-18).

Define *jealousy*:

Of whom are you jealous?

• What do these people have that you want, and why?

How has jealousy affected your relationships with these people?

• How has it affected your self-esteem?

• How do ingratitude and comparison stoke the fire of jealousy?

Acceptance

Having admitted our powerlessness over chemical substances, we have taken a giant step in the road toward acceptance. Simply knowing that we are in God's will by being in recovery shows that we are progressing in the acceptance of our circumstances.

As we grow with him, we learn that He may call upon us to do seemingly small things which are really most important. One young man who has been recovering from alcohol and drug addiction for six years said: "I used to think of 'God's will' as something grand and glorious. Maybe that's the case for some people, but when I was getting sober, His will for me was to stay out of convenience stores. Those stores were always trouble for me because I could never stop without buying a six-pack of beer. It was a simple assignment," he said, "but at the same time, a very great task.

Gradually, as we continue to walk with God, we'll be able to accept whatever place He puts us in – socially, economically, relationally, and circumstantially – because there is no peace like that which comes from being in His will. And God's peace *surpasses all comprehension* (Phil. 4:7).

How do gratitude and contentment encourage a sense of peace and acceptance?

How are you expressing and experiencing acceptance?

What factors are hindering the experience of acceptance in your life?

What factors are encouraging your experience of acceptance?

What changes might you expect if you fully accept each challenge the Lord gives you?

Read Ps. 73:25. What was the source of Asaph's contentment?

- How can you apply this to your life?

Criticism

Here, we are not thinking of the positive advice we offer when asked, but that negative judgment of ourselves and others that is rooted in pride, in our need to be perfect or to be perceived as such.

Usually, criticism takes the form of verbal abuse, but sometimes, it can be more subtle masked in sarcasm or silence.

There are many reasons why we are critical. One is that we often see others as a reflection of ourselves. Criticism thus becomes a form of control which motivates others to conform to our standards.

We put other people down to elevate ourselves. This is usually the result of a low sense of self-worth and the false belief: *Those who fail are unworthy of love and deserve to be punished.*

Sometimes, we are critical because we truly believe others need our guidance. We perceive that our correction will be beneficial to them. Later, we are surprised to realize that these people avoid us because our habit of "correcting" has been more destructive than constructive to them.

Scripture admonishes us to ...*encourage one another, and build up one another*... (1 Thess. 5:11), and tells us that we are to ...*love one another, for love is from God ... if God so loved us, we also ought to love one another* (1 John 4:7,11).

As two writers have said: "People need love, especially when they don't deserve it,"[2]and, "He who seeks a friend without a fault remains without one."[3]

We would do well to remember to pray for others as often as we are tempted to criticize them.

Why do you criticize other people? What results do you expect?

In what ways do you communicate criticism to others?

How does a critical attitude affect your relationships?

How does it affect you?

Love

When we consider *love,* we may think of the warm exuberance, queasiness, restlessness, and sense of anticipation we feel toward another person when "falling in love." Fortunately, these emotional feelings, experienced at the onset of *attraction,* do not comprise the full context of love because feelings like these tend to ebb and flow.

God ordained love to be a lasting attitude comprised of action, and He who goes before us in all things has given us the example we are to follow in this area. John 3:16 says: "God *so loved* the world that He *gave* His only Son..." Jesus said in John 15:13: "Greater *love* has no one than this, that one *lay down* his life for his friends." Titus 3:4-5 says, "But when the kindness of God our Savior and His *love* for mankind appeared, He *saved us*, not on the basis of deeds which we have done in righteousness, but according to His mercy, *by the washing of regeneration* and *renewing by the Holy Spirit."*

God's love for us is not based on His emotions, but is demonstrated by His actions. As we grow in our understanding of His love and mercy toward us, we will increasingly desire to demonstrate our love for Him and others actively and in obedience to these commands:

> *You shall love the Lord your God with all your heart, and with all your soul, and with all   your mind.*
> *This is the great and foremost commandment.*
> *And a second is like it, You shall love your neighbor as yourself.*
> *On these two commandments depend the whole Law and the Prophets.*
> (Matt. 22:37-40)

Perhaps the best way we can measure our growth in the area of love is to examine what Paul wrote to the Corinthian believers on this subject:

> *Love is patient, love is kind, and is not jealous; love does not brag and is not arrogant,*
> *(love) does not act unbecomingly; it does not seek its own, is not provoked, does not take   into account a wrong suffered,*
> *does not rejoice in unrighteousness, but rejoices with the truth;*
> *(love) bears all things, believes all things, hopes all things, endures all things.*
> *Love never fails...*
> **But now abides faith, hope, love, these three: but the greatest of these if**
> **love.**
> (1 Cor. 13:4-8,13)

Complete the following statement:

Love is...

List some ways people normally express love:

What does it mean to *love your neighbor as yourself?*

• How are you expressing love for others?

• For yourself?

What do you think it means to *love the Lord your God with all your heart, soul, and mind?*

How are you expressing love for God...

• With your heart?

• With your mind?

• With your soul?

How has Christ demonstrated His love for us?

How does experiencing His love help you to love others?

Contrast the effects of love and criticism?

Example:

Love	Criticism

Sexual Behavior

God, our Creator, fashioned every part of our bodies, including our nerve impulses and sexual responses (Ps. 119:73; 139:13). Our sexuality is His gift to us, ordained by Him for procreation (reproduction) and for our good pleasure. Pleasure, as C.S. Lewis once observed, is God's invention, not Satan's. [4]

Concerning procreation, God wanted to ensure that we would be compelled to preserve the human race by "bearing fruit and multiplying." If this was His intent, many of us will agree that He did a good job, given the seemingly overpowering sexual urges we all experience from time to time.

But why pleasure? We have only to look at the surroundings He provided Adam and Eve in the Garden of Eden to understand that God's original intent for man included his enjoyment of the earth and all it contained (Gen. 2:8-17). It was Adam, remember, who distorted this plan by rebelling against God. As his descendants, we continue to bear the consequences of Adam's original sin.

But the point is, God fully intends for us to enjoy sexual pleasure within the constraints of the marital union, and this for at least three reasons:

- *The pleasure of sexual union serves as a reminder of the exquisite joy we will experience when we, as believers (called His "bride"), will be joined together with Him, "the bridegroom"* (see Matt. 9:14-15; 25:1-3; John 3:28-29; Rev. 19:7). The marital union itself was created as a symbol of our relationship with God. Our union with Him is one which He has promised will never be broken, regardless of our behavior. To those who receive Him as Lord, He is faithful (see Deut. 7:9).

- *Because God made us, He knows under what conditions we will be at our best.* He created our sexuality for the safe, trusting confines of marriage, not for promiscuity. When we rebel and pervert this plan, we bring upon ourselves devastating consequences: a negative self-image; the pain of a broken relationship and sometimes, a broken home; marital distrust, shattered lives, distorted perceptions about sex and members of the opposite sex; and in some cases, even death.

- *Sex is ordained for marriage for the sake of children.* If adult lives are shattered by sexual misconduct, what about its impact on children? Some children, victims of rape, incest, or simply a broken parental relationship, carry emotional scars into adulthood that haunt them all their lives. Sometimes, these scars are borne out in compulsive behaviors like eating disorders, physical abuse, excessive masturbation, alcoholism, drug and/or sexual addiction. (Some also suffer from a loss of sexual function or desire, and some develop a same-sex sexual orientation as a result of these traumas.)

Sexual sin is manifested in many ways: premarital sex, adultery, homosexuality, pornography, exhibitionism, voyeurism, fetishism, pedophilia, sadism, masochism, incest, and necrophilia, among others.

The scope of this book is not such that we can address these issues in detail. Nor do we wish to further burden our readers with added guilt and shame. We condemn sexual deviation; we do not condemn sinners like ourselves.

The point is this: we may have been involved in one or more sexual sins before our addiction, but drinking or using may have compounded our moral laxity. As we have mentioned before, when chemical substances are released into the body, they go to work on the central nervous system. One of many results is a relaxing of inhibitions which often results in relaxed values.

Whatever our behavior before and during our addiction, we need to draw it out into God's light and love, and be reconciled to Him through His loving forgiveness.

What are some ways our culture distorts our God-given sexuality?

If you have misused your sexuality in any of the ways already mentioned, how has this harmed others? Be specific:

Example:

Person (first name only)	Result

How has sexual misbehavior harmed you?
- Has it affected your self-esteem? If so, how?

Read 1 Cor. 6:9-20. What does God desire for this are of your life?

Are you taking any steps to fulfill His desire for you? If so, what are they?

- If not, why are you withholding this area of your life from Him?

- What do you need to enable you to surrender your sexuality to God?

STEP FIVE

We admit to God, to ourselves, and to another human being the exact nature of our wrongs.

Therefore, confess your sins to one another, and pray for one another, so that you may be healed. (James 5:16a)

"The Serenity Prayer" is one that is popular among those recovering from chemical dependency, and in it we find some good advice:

> *God grant me the serenity*
> *To accept the things I cannot change,*
> *Courage to change the things I can,*
> *And wisdom to know the difference.*

There are many things about our lives that we cannot change. We cannot change our past, nor can we change the fact that we are chemically dependent. Happily, serenity does not begin with change. It begins with acceptance.

Step 5 is one through which we can discover the joy, peace, and relief that comes with acceptance. In it, we find the principle that as we reconciled to God, we are reconciled to our fellow man.

The CROP Process

When it comes to opposing the strongholds in your life, I can think of no better acronym for you to remember than C-R-O-P. Each of the letters of CROP represents a step in the four-stage process of eliminating the undesirable things in your life: *Confession, Repentance, Obedience, and Praise*. If bitterness is "part of the picture," you can CROP it out. And any other strongholds can also be demolished in order to help you focus more clearly on the positive aspects you want to emphasize.

Confession. We've tried to destroy our strongholds our own way and wind up saddled with bitterness and unforgiveness. Confess literally means "to agree with God." We need to agree with God that our strongholds are evil. We need to acknowledge our sinful behavior as a major obstacle on our road to freedom.

Most Christians don't understand confession. Those who comprehend it only partially understand it. I know this has been my case. I believed that confession entailed agreeing with God as to the reality of sin in my life. But that was the extent of it.

76

Suppose I told a lie. I could then agree with God that I had indeed lied, ask him to forgive me, and I would feel that I had completed the act of confession. But with this system of easy confession, I would find it pretty easy to lie again.

True confession of sin is more than agreeing with God about the *actuality* of sin. It must go beyond and help us to realize the reality of sin's destructiveness. Until we see evil for what it is, we will never understand the full depth of God's forgiveness.

Connie had been used and abused. She felt her hatred of certain other people was both justified and reasonable. But her hatred spread quickly until it was no longer isolated to those who had hurt her. The least offense against her, even by those who wanted to help, would immediately bring down her wrath on them. People learned to keep their distance, and Connie concluded that God was ultimately responsible for all the pains that she had experienced.

One day she was in a group where she was encouraged to speak about her feelings toward God. Out of her mouth came a litany of foul language that shocked her. For the first time she realized how holding on to the hatred of others had poisoned her very soul. Once she saw the true nature of her sin, she wanted to be released from it.

When I first learned to confess my sin, I sat under a tree with a sheet of paper and made a long list. I soon discovered that this was much too quick – that there was considerably more involved. The steps that follow in the CROP process will not lead to freedom unless confession is complete. I don't mean that you must recall every single wrong thing you've ever done before you can move on. Rather, as God reveals an area of sin to you, do not move on to the next step until you have seen how destructive this sin has been.

In addition to helping us see the destructiveness of our sin, confession helps us by revealing the connectiveness of our sins. I may be confessing, for example, the sin of lying. God may show me how my lying is connected to pride or a need to keep everyone pleased with me. Or the lying may be a "screen" to keep some other area of life from exposure. Our sins are usually connected to other sins. If we allow God to show us the connections, we can clear out a network of evil from our lives.

With confession we are dependent on the Holy Spirit to show us: (1) our surface sins, (2) how each sin might be connected to other sins, and (3) the extent of destructive evil in our lives due to our sins. Attempting to discern these things apart from the Holy Spirit will only lead into morbid introspection and the unveiling of hurts that will not be comforted.

Many counselors, however, believe that anything you can uncover must need uncovering. Without the guidance of the Holy Spirit, a counselor can lead a person through tremendous torment. We don't need to uncover everything in confession – just what God reveals. He knows exactly how much we are capable of handling.

Repentance. Our relationship with God is equally important in the second step of the CROP process – repentance. The concept of repentance is one of "turning back." Through repentance we turn from our self-willed approach to life and reestablished a face-to-face relationship with Jesus.

We often think repentance involves promising to do something to become more worthwhile to God. By focusing on our performance, however, we miss out on what it really means to be in a relationship. When we truly relate to God, we can do no less than relate to him as Lord. We must accept his leadership in our lives through the Holy Spirit.

Some people find it hard to accept such a complete yielding to God, especially those who have lived with great hurt in their lives. For many of us, the priority list of life goes something like this:

1. Air
2. Water
3. Food
4. Control

Ironically, the more we need to control, the less control we have. Fear begins to rule because we feel that if we lose control something bad will happen to us, something hurtful, so we refuse to yield to anyone – including God. As a result, we're saddled with all the fears and hurts that go along with such a great responsibility.

We who have lost the ability to trust others find repentance a difficult step. Trust is a precious commodity. But the challenge held out to us is this, "Taste and see that the Lord is good; blessed is the man who takes refuge in him" (Ps 34:8). Through repentance we "turn back" the control of our lives to God. He's the only one capable of handling it without all the hurts and fears that would otherwise result.

Associated with repentance is reliance. All our lives we have relied on the patterns of our childhood. We cannot be in a state where we are not reliant on something or someone. We will rely either on the patterns of our flesh, or the guidance of the Spirit. Scripture states this clearly in Galatians 5:16 when it says, "Walk by the Spirit and you will not carry out the desires of the flesh" (NAS). Unfortunately, we often try to turn from something without turning to the God who can set us free. Pray for the courage and faith that only God can give so that you can repent and rely on God.

Obedience. Our confession and repentance must come out of a viable relationship with God. The same is true about the third step of obedience. But in this case, we need to turn our attention to God's power.

By the time we discover strongholds in our lives, we also see that we are incapable of doing away with them using our own power. If we are to discover what God can do through us, we must learn to respond to him differently than we have in the past. If we have failed to respond to him, or have responded in wrong ways, we need to change how we relate to him.

Many of us have no confidence in our ability to respond differently. We groan at the thought. In addition, some of us have strong negative perceptions of obedience. We think obedience means having to do something against our wills or facing the consequences. But if our confession and repentance are genuine, we should see things from God's perspective. Obedience shouldn't seem like such an unpleasant alternative. It's a change of response that we should be more than willing to undertake.

If we have prepared through true confession and repentance, we have trapped into God's power to confront the darkness of our souls. Now it's only natural to want to keep the relationship strong as we seek to overcome the darkness and evil.

Does this mean our battle against evil is won – over and done with? Not by a long shot. That's why obedience is such an important step. Continued obedience results in continued victory. But it's easy to revert to our old, self-centered ways. When we seek to take back the control of our lives, we set ourselves up for failure. Yet God is quick to forgive us when we see the error of our ways and turn back to him.

Recall the incident of Peter's walking on the water to meet Jesus (see Matthew 14:22-33). Peter was able to show faith in Jesus to the extent that he walked across the water to meet him. What an amazing example of trust and obedience! But what happened? Peter took his focus off Jesus and transferred it to the circumstances around him – the wind, the waves, and the fact that he was standing on top of the water.

Yet if I'm going to make mistakes in life, I want them to be like Peter's. It is said, "To fail, you must first try." Jesus gently chided Peter for "little faith," yet it was clear that the reason Peter failed was because he had tried something others were unwilling to do. When the disciples got back to shore, at least Peter had gotten his feet wet.

When it comes to obedience, we can learn by trying even if we fail. *Notice that Peter was not punished for his failure*. Jesus reached out and lifted him up. A far worse mistake is to refuse to change how we respond to God and fall back into the same patterns that have always controlled us.

Confession. Repentance. Obedience. These things are difficult to get started. They require a new and different way of relating to God. Yet once we start, they begin a cycle of freedom that replaces the cycle of bondage caused by our previous patterns.

Praise. We are commanded throughout Scripture to offer praise and give thanks to God. Sometimes praise comes naturally. When things go our way, we rejoice and are thankful. But how about those times when we're feeling pain or depression? During those times praise is definitely not natural.

I believe praise is the highest form of spiritual warfare. David wrote: "You are enthroned as the Holy One; You are the praise of Israel" (Ps 22:3). After genuine confession, repentance, and obedience, praise is not optional – it's automatic. The first three steps will produce freedom from our strongholds and an overriding sense of freedom in our lives. As we experience this freedom that only God can provide, our hearts will praise him.

The CROP process, from start to finish, seeks change in our lives by changing and correcting our relationship with God. Consequently, the results are real and lasting. We can do no less than praise him.

Going Through the CROP Process

It may be difficult to theorize how the four-step CROP process works, so let's walk through the process with a specific example. Since bitterness may be the root of the other strongholds, let's see how we might go about getting rid of it.

Confessing Bitterness. Many of us are blinded to how many of the significant events in our lives can be traced back to bitterness. So we need to pray that God will search our hearts and find anything that might be there. As we yield to the illumination of the Holy Spirit, we might recall events we have not thought of in years. Again, it's not important for us to "rack our brains" in attempting to remember everything. Allow the Holy Spirit to bring the truth to light.

It's also important not to argue with the Spirit when such things are revealed. Our first instinct will be to defend our actions. Often, due to hatred and self-pity, we give ourselves permission to react in destructive ways – rebellion, drug use, sexual activity, withdrawal, self-will, or passivity. All these things are connected to bitterness, and we need to deal with each stronghold.

Ask the Holy Spirit to show you how these responses have destroyed or limited your life. Take your time. Unless you experience with God what these improper responses have done to your life, you will not be ready to go forward. When God says you have seen enough and you have confessed these things, *then* you are ready to go the next step.

Repenting of bitterness. Bitterness and its related behaviors are the products of a self-willed life. The thought of living any other way will be frightening. You may have heard about, talked about, and sung about the lordship of Christ for most of your life. But at this stage, when you actually begin to experience it, you may experience a sensation of death within your soul. You are, in fact, putting to death your old ways of responding to life. This will feel uncomfortable and frightening at first.

Yet you'll quickly discover that the fear of the Lord is by no means as discomforting as the other fears you've had – fears of inadequacy, of the unknown, and of never being able to eliminate the pain you're feeling. As we repent and turn back toward God, there will be an awesomeness about the experience. We clearly see who we are only by first seeing who he is.

Obedience as a replacement for bitterness. Much of our behavior is not what it should be due to the bitterness we have harbored for so long. Consequently, this might be a lengthy and difficult step. God has shown us the problem areas and we have repented of them by agreeing that they are wrong and seeing the extent of their destructive influence. But now we have to replace each of those errant behaviors with obedience to God.

In some cases, we already know what we're supposed to do. In other instances, however, we might need to continue to search God's Word and seek his will for how to stop being so bitter. Again, take your time. God does not reveal problems without also revealing solutions. As we begin to conform to his will in the ways we know how, we will begin to see what we need to do in the other areas as well. It is through obedience that you see God's complete power over the stronghold of bitterness, as well as the work he has already accomplished in your life.

Praise for victory over bitterness. The struggle against bitterness has been a long and difficult one, even with God's help. It has taken time and energy to see the extent of the effects of bitterness in your life. It has been painful to repent of each of these things. Replacing improper behaviors with godly ones has taken a lot of effort as well. But it has all been worth it.

When you experience release from the devastating weight of bitterness, joy will fill your soul. Lightness will accompany your step. Praise will flow from your lips. The newfound feeling of freedom will affect everything you do.

You don't have to understand it. You *can't* understand it. Just enjoy it and appreciate it. "Do not be anxious about anything, but in everything, by prayer and petition, with thanksgiving, present your requests to God. And the peace of God, which transcends all understanding, will guard your hearts and your minds in Christ Jesus" (Phil 4:6-7).

Putting it all Together

Going through the CROP process will probably be difficult at first. You'll be dealing with things you haven't done anything about for years. But as you begin to use the steps of Confession, Repentance, Obedience, and Praise on a regular basis, the process won't seem nearly as cumbersome.

Since you're following the same pattern, you'll quickly become accustomed to going through the steps. What follows are some sample prayers that reflect the CROP process. While these samples are abbreviated, you can see that after your initial struggles to see your strongholds fall, the CROP steps can be short and effective. I have filled the blanks with sample answers. You can substitute your own to fit your circumstances.

Lord Jesus, I have *(hated)* my *(mom)* because she *(shouted at me)*. I agree with you that this is sin. Thank you for forgiving me. I now destroy this stronghold of *(hate)* in the name of the Lord Jesus Christ. I now choose, by my own free will, to forgive *(my mom)* for *(shouting at me)*. From now on, when I remember *(my mom shouting at me)*, I will choose to remember *(her)* as forgiven. Thank you for the truth that is setting me free.

Lord Jesus, I have *(been self-righteous and I think I am superior to others)*. I agree with you that this is sin. Thank you for forgiving me. I now destroy this stronghold of *(self-righteousness)* in the name of the Lord Jesus Christ. Thank you for the truth that sets me free.

Lord Jesus, I have *(been rebellious against my dad)*. I agree with you that this is sin. Thank you for providing the truth that sets me free.

Lord Jesus, I choose, by my own free will, to forgive myself for *(adultery)* because you have forgiven me. Thank you that your truth is setting me free.

Lord Jesus, I acknowledge that I have *(participated in asking questions using a Quija Board)*. This is sin. I renounce this act. Thank you for forgiving me. I now consider this stronghold destroyed in the name of Jesus.

Lord Jesus, I have allowed myself to feel *(hopeless in my marriage)* – this is sin. You have told me my hope is in you. Thank you for forgiving me. I now destroy the stronghold of *(hopelessness)*.

As you can see, the CROP steps follow a definite pattern. But the actual language and expression is up to you. Make it personal. Mean what you say. And don't stop until your strongholds have fallen.

Where are the Weapons?

In the previous discussion of 2 Corinthians 10:3-5, I said I would tell you about "the weapons we fight with" which "are not the weapons of the world." By now you may be wondering: *What are these special weapons that have "divine power," and where can I acquire an arsenal of my own?*

The only weapons you need are the ones just described in this chapter: confession, repentance, obedience, and praise. These are more than nice habits practiced by good people. When handled correctly, they are weapons. No stronghold – not even Satan himself – can stand against them. If you make the CROP process a regular practice in your life, you should see your strongholds begin to fall.

Can you again be victimized by your strongholds? From now on, that will be up to you. Strongholds can only be formed when you let a problem go unattended for a long period of time. When you were younger, you didn't know any better. Your strongholds took advantage of your childhood patterns, your fears, and your desire to avoid pain at any price. Now that you can see things a bit more clearly, you can eliminate those strongholds. They will try to come back. However, you will have destroyed the power of Satan in those stronghold areas.

This time you should notice when the strongholds begin to form again. You already know the terrible amounts of pain they will cause if you don't do something. And you have an effective four-step process (CROP) to do away with them. So as long as you continue to draw on God's power to face down your strongholds, they should never regain control.

And do you know what? You're going to experience the freedom God has been wanting you to have all along! You will finally be able to know what Jesus meant when he said we could have "life, and have it to the full" (Jn 10:10). By leaving your bondage behind, you will be entering a fresh new life. Your long search for freedom is finally going to see some results.

Choosing a Good Listener

With a better understanding of what it means to confess our wrongs to God, we are ready to analyze the best way to complete a successful fifth step. We begin by determining who will be the best person for us to talk with. Choosing a good listener; choosing the *right* listener is imperative for a good fifth step. In fact, this choice should be made only after prayerful consideration.

The following may be of help to you in your selection process. We urge you to pray for this person with these guidelines in mind:

Choose someone who has spent several years in recovery, or who is very familiar with both the fifth step and the issues of chemical dependency. Step 5 is a life-or-death errand; it can mean the difference between recovery and returning to addiction. A person who is familiar with this step, with recovery, or with dependency issues will understand its importance for you and your recovery.

82

Choose someone who can keep a confidence. The information you are preparing to disclose is very personal. The person you select to talk with should be completely trustworthy in this respect.

Choose an objective listener. This is not yet the time (it may never be) to talk openly with those who are emotionally involved with us, and who may find what we have to say more than they can bear. Be considerate in this respect. Sharing is a responsibility.

Choose someone who may be willing to share personal examples from his or her life with you. The person you talk with should be a good listener, but it is often through and exchange that you will find the acceptance you especially need right now.

- List some people who might be good listeners for you:

- How will you choose the person best for you to talk with?

- When will you talk to him or her?

Telling a Story

Once we have found a good listener, we are ready to get on with the telling. We have found that this works best as a story, the story of our lives.

Perhaps the best way to begin is by taking some notes, starting from the very beginning and including those persons, circumstances, and events that have affected you most along the way. You will, of course, want to refer back continually to your fourth step to interject *all* the significant things you have done – positive and negative – over the years.

When you do finally sit down with the person you've chosen – your sponsor, pastor, counselor, physician, or trusted friend – you may want to read from your notes, or refer back to them as an outline. This is up to you. The point is to get it ALL out; everything that is significant about your life that has never been said.

We leave you to write your story with some final words of caution: It has been our experience that some people who took the fifth step were disappointed because they experienced no immediate feeling of gratification afterward. A successful fifth step is not determined by feelings, but by disclosing the significant events in your life which need to be shared with another human being. We urge you to think on this *before* you take this step so that you can be realistic in your expectations.

Finally, it should be remembered that this step is for *you.* Regardless of whom we choose to share ourselves with, it is imperative to realize that our purpose in taking this step is NOT to please the listener, but to gain healing for ourselves.

Story Outline

What was your life like when you were a child? (Describe your relationships with your parents, brothers, and sisters):

Describe how your home life has affected you:

When did you first try alcohol or drugs?

- Why did you start?

Go back through the questions in step four, and explain in detail how chemical substances have effected…

- your self-esteem:

- your relationship s with your family:

- your relationships with your friends:

- your jobs:

- your values:

List some of the significant events described in your fourth step:

STEP SIX

We commit ourselves to obedience to God, desiring that He remove patterns of sin from our lives.

Humble yourselves in the presence of the Lord, and He will exalt you. (James 4:10)

When we came into treatment or recovery, it may have been for one of two reasons: we either were confronted with our behavior and couldn't escape the obvious facts pointing to our addiction or we were experiencing physical and/or emotional pain as a result of our addiction. We wanted relief. What we *really* wanted was to be rid of the negative side effects that accompanied our addiction. We wanted the people around us to change. We wanted to feel better physically. We wanted to be relieved of our "anxiety." We thought that *these* problems were the source of our troubles. When confronted with our behavior, our addiction, and the issue of abstinence, we were less than enchanted.

It is much the same when we come to the cross of Christ to commit ourselves in obedience to Him. We may be happy to know Jesus as our *Savior* because of the many blessings that accompany salvation: receiving His love, forgiveness, complete acceptance, and gift of eternal life. But when we begin to consider submitting ourselves to Him as our *Lord,* many of us hesitate. Why?

Even as Christians, we still may be uncertain that God is capable of transforming our lives. We lack faith in His resurrection power. In addition, we may feel that we are unworthy of the love He gives, which can so drastically change our lives. We may also have misperceptions about the true character of God. These can lead to wrong motives in both serving Him and seeking Him as our source for healing. Finally, we may be trying to achieve spiritual growth through our own determination and willpower, rather than relying on the Holy Spirit, our source of change.

Let's examine each of these to discover where we are now in our relationship with God:

Lack of Faith
Read the eleventh chapter of Hebrews.

- From this chapter, give a brief definition of faith:

- What account of faith given here impresses you most, and why?

- To what area of your life can you apply this example of faith?

Read Rom. 10:8-17. What do you learn from this passage about acquiring faith?

85

Read Col. 1:15-20; Phil. 2:9-11; Heb. 2:14-15; 4:15. From these passages, give some reasons why we can depend on Jesus Christ as our source of strength and obedience:

- How can His authority and power over evil help you to resist temptation and stand firm in obedience?

Read Is. 7:7,9 and Eph. 6:10-18.

- Why is faith so important in our battle against evil?

- How does a shield protect the warrior in battle?

- In what practical ways can you *take up the shield of faith* in your life?

Read Luke 11:5-13 with Luke 18:1-8.

- How do the man's persistence in Luke 11 and the woman's persistence in Luke 18 prove their faith?

- How do *asking, seeking,* and *knocking* demonstrate faith?

- What are the strengths and weaknesses of your relationship with God at this point in your life?

Example:

Strengths	Weaknesses

- In what areas of your life do you need to be more persistent (or faithful)?

- What factors would help you both to persist and to grow in your relationship with God? (Consider supportive relationships, honesty, the Scriptures, the Holy Spirit, specific choices and habits, time).

Feelings of Unworthiness
Read Luke 7:36-48,50.

- If we liken the Pharisees in this passage to our society today, what is the difference between the Lord's view of sinners and society's view?

86

- Do you think Jesus finds it harder to forgive "big sins" than "little sins"?

- This woman's heart was filled with gratitude toward Jesus in response to His love for her. She demonstrated her gratitude in action. In what practical ways can we demonstrate our gratitude to the Lord Jesus in our daily lives?

Misunderstanding the True Character of God

The following is a list of attitudes about God and relating to Him that are shared by many people who are codependent and/or chemically dependent. We will examine these as they relate to persons who are chemically dependent:[1]

- *God is mean.* Many of us don't believe that God has our best interests at heart. Perhaps we have seen others tangibly reap God's blessings, while nothing good seems to be happening in our own lives. We may have thus concluded that God loves others, but only wants to punish us.

  Some of us believe that God wants to rob us rather than enrich us. This is one of Satan's ploys. When he appeared to Eve in the Garden of Eden, he didn't say, "Wow! Look at all these trees you can eat from! God has certainly blessed you!" Instead, he focused her attention on the one tree that was forbidden to her (see Gen. 3:5-6). He does the same today by drawing our attention to the restrictions rather than the blessings of Christian living.[2]

- *The Lord demands too much of me.* One of the reasons dependent persons use or drink is to escape responsibility. Life's duties seem frightening when we're sober. Add to our daily responsibilities the burden of obedience, and many of us may feel overwhelmed.

- *I don't want to lose control of my life.* Those who are dependent are often slow to grasp the truth about "control." Although we can see improvements in our lives as a result of relinquishing that which we thought was enabling us to be in control — chemical substances — we can't seem to transfer this concept to other areas of our lives. We may even be willing to admit that we gained a new sense of control over our lives when we stopped drinking or using. Yet we continue to hedge on allowing Christ to rule our lives, still unable to grasp that *His* control is our ticket to freedom.

- *I don't want to be perceived as weird.* Many of us have been isolated from true intimacy and companionship by the numbing, excluding effects of our dependency. Some of us still haven't developed friendships with people outside of our former drinking or using circle. Add to these circumstances that fact that we may feel alone as a recovering dependent, and the result is that we are terrified of how others will respond if we take a stand for Christ in our daily affairs.

Which of the above attitudes do you see in your own life? What causes you to feel this way?

It is important to understand that all of these attitudes are misperceptions. Take a moment now to tell God how you are feeling by putting your thoughts in writing. Then ask Him to convey His truth to you as you have opportunities to trust Him in the months ahead.

Examining the Truth

In this exercise, we will examine some truths about God.

Read John 1:17-18; 14:8-10. How can you know the truth regarding God's character?

Christ perfectly reveals the Father to us. What does each of these passages teach you about Christ?

- John 4:13-18,39
- John 10:15
- John 14:2-3
- John 15:13-15
- John 17:23

Using the content of the previous passages of Scripture, write a few sentences explaining how God relates to you and feels about you.

I know that my heavenly Father...

Read Psalm 103. In the left column, write characteristics of God the Father that you see in this psalm. In the right column, write out what difference this characteristic makes in your life.

Example:

My heavenly Father is...	*As a result I...*

It is critical that we accurately know the one true God. We will only follow someone whom we know and trust. Satan deceives us by distorting the character of God: *If you follow and obey God, you'll be miserable. God does not love you because you did this. God won't accept someone like you.* By deceiving us about God's love and power, Satan robs us of the desire to love, obey, and honor Him.

How can we overcome the subtle deceptions of the enemy? Paul wrote that we are to be transformed by the renewing of our minds (Rom. 12:2), but we cannot combat the *spiritual forces of wickedness* (Eph. 6:12) with our own human resources. Nor can we experience transformation in accordance with God's will through intellectual enlightenment or the power of positive thinking. Scripture says: *You are from God, little children, and have overcome them* (demonic forces); *because greater is He who is in you than he who is in the world* (1 John 4:4). The work of our transformation is God's, and He accomplishes that work through the One who comes to reside within us at the moment of our spiritual birth: the Holy Spirit.

The Holy Spirit

The Holy Spirit, the third Person of the Trinity, is God and possesses all the attributes of deity. His primary purpose is to glorify Christ and bring attention to Him. Christ said, "He shall glorify Me; for He shall take of mine, and shall disclose it to you" (John 16:14). The Holy Spirit is our teacher, and He guides us into the truth of the Scriptures (John 16:13). It is His power that the love of Christ flows through us and produces spiritual fruit within us (John 7:37-39; 15:1-8).

In Gal. 5:22, this spiritual fruit is described as *love, joy, peace, patience, kindness, goodness, faithfulness, gentleness, self-control.* In other passages in the New Testament, it is described as *intimate friendship with Christ* (John 15:14); *love for one another* (John 15:12); *joy and peace in the midst of difficulties* (John 14:27; 15:11); *steadfastness* (1 Cor. 15:58); *singing, thankfulness, and submission* (Eph. 5:18-21); and *evangelism and discipleship* (Matt. 28:18-20).

Reading this, we may initially feel dismayed, realizing that many of these qualities are absent from our lives – whether we've known the Lord for a long time or not.

We must remember that Christianity is not a self-improvement program (as are so many programs in our culture today.). Nor is our goal perfection. When perfection is our aim, we become prideful and are motivated to perform by rules. This is not God's intent, nor should it be ours. Our goal is *progress.* We are making progress when we draw on Christ as our resource for direction, encouragement, and strength.

To better understand this, let's look at what Jesus said in John 15:1, 4-5:

I am the true vine, and My Father is the vine dresser.
...Abide in (live, grow, and gain your sustenance from) *Me, and I in you. As the branch cannot bear fruit of itself, unless it abides in the vine, so neither can you, unless you abide in Me.*
I am the vine, you are the branches; he who abides in Me, and I in him, he bears much fruit; for apart from Me you can do nothing.

89

Nothing? Yes, in terms of that which is honoring to Christ, is spiritually nourishing to us, and is genuine Christian service, anything done apart from the love and power of Christ amounts to nothing. Although we may expend tremendous effort at a great personal cost, only that which is done for Christ's glory and in the power of His Spirit is of eternal value. The very power of God that was evident when Christ was raised from the dead (Eph. 1:19-21) is available to every believer who abides in Him, who desires that He be honored, and who trusts that His Spirit will produce fruit in his or her life.

The Battle Within

How can we begin to experience the Holy Spirit's power in our lives? First, we must understand that as Christians, a continual battle is working within us. Each time we move toward the cross to do those things that are pleasing to God, our "flesh," or human nature, compels us to retreat. On the other hand, when we begin to venture toward sin, the Holy Spirit prompts us to obey.

But I say, walk by the Spirit, and you will not carry out the desire of the flesh.
For the flesh sets its desires against the Spirit, and the Spirit against the flesh; for these are in opposition to one another, so that you may not do the things that you please.
(Gal. 5:16-17)

For I know that nothing good dwells in me, that is, in my flesh; for the wishing is present in me, but the doing of the good is not.
For the good that I wish, I do not do; but I practice the very evil that I do not wish.
I find then the principle that evil is present in me, the one who wishes to do good.
For I joyfully concur with the law of God in the inner man,
but I see a different law in the members of my body, waging war against the law of my mind, and making me a prisoner of the law of sin which is in my members.
(Rom. 7:18-19, 21-23)

In addition to this struggle we face against our own flesh, we are also in a continual battle as God's elect against Satan and his unseen forces. As Paul wrote to the believers in Ephesus:

For our struggle is not against flesh and blood, but against the rulers, against the powers, against the world forces of this darkness, against the spiritual forces of wickedness in the heavenly places. (Eph. 6:12)

The only way we can hope to achieve victory over these struggles is through the power of the Holy Spirit.

The following exercise will help you understand how God can empower you to live according to His truth by depending on His Spirit to complete the work He has started within you (Phil. 1:6).

Read John 7:37-39 and answer the following questions:

- *If any man is thirsty* is a metaphor for our desire and need for Christ. What does it mean to *drink* of Christ?

- In what ways are you *thirsty* for Him?

- What are some aspects of the Christian life that *rivers of living water* might symbolize?

- Jesus said that these "rivers" flow from our *innermost being.* What does this mean to you?

Read John 15:1-8. This passage contains another metaphor which illustrates that the Holy Spirit is the source of a life that honors Christ. Answer the following:

- Describe how a branch produces fruit (vv. 4-5):

- What are some evidences of spiritual *fruit* within the believer's life?

- John 15:2 says that God prunes every fruitful branch, that it may bear more fruit. Can you think of some ways God might *prune* us?

- What are some things that prevent a branch from producing fruit?

- What could prevent you from living a more fruitful, Christ-honoring life?

- Summarize Christ's teaching in these two passages (John 7:37; 39; 15:1-8) in your own words:

We can't accomplish God's will by self-effort; the Holy Spirit gives us the wisdom and the strength to turn from sin and walk with God in obedience. At the same time, God does not act alone. We experience His victory as we cooperate with Him. Our part is to be responsive and responsible. His part is to work in and through us as Paul wrote the Colossian believers: *And for this purpose also I labor, striving according to His power which mightily works within me* (Col. 1:19).

In the following exercise, we will examine six biblical motives for choosing to cooperate with God by acting in obedience, rather than choosing to live in sin and self-effort.

Motivations for Obedience

God's love and acceptance of us is based on His grace, His unmerited favor, not on our ability to impress Him through our good deeds. But if we are accepted on the basis of His grace and not our deeds, why *should* we obey God? According to scriptural principles, there are at least six proper motivations for obedience:

91

Christ's Love

When we experience love, we usually respond by seeking to express our love in return. Our obedience to God is an expression of our love for Him (John 14:15, 21), which comes from an understanding of what Christ has accomplished for us on the cross (2 Cor. 5:14-15). We love because He first loved us and clearly demonstrated His love for us at the cross (1 John 4:16-19).

This great motivating factor is missing in many of our lives because we don't really believe that God loves us unconditionally. We expect His love to be conditional, based on our ability to earn it.

Our experience of God's love is based on our perception. If we believe that He is demanding or aloof, we will not experience His love and tenderness. Instead, we will either be afraid of Him or angry with Him. Faulty perceptions of God often prompt us to rebel against Him.

Our image of God is the foundation for all of our motivations. As we grow in our understanding of His unconditional love and acceptance, we will increasingly want our lives to bring honor to the One who loves us so much.

Does the love of Christ compel you to obey Him? Why, or why not?

Sin is Destructive

Satan has effectively blinded man to the painful, damaging consequences of sin. The effects of sin are all around us, yet many continue to indulge in the pleasure-seeking and rampart self-centeredness that causes so much anguish and pain. Satan contradicted God in the Garden when he said, "You surely shall not die!" (Gen. 3:4). Sin is pleasant, but only for a season. Sooner or later, it will result in some form of destruction.

Sin is destructive in many ways. Emotionally, we can experience guilt and shame as well as the fears of failure and punishment. Mentally, we may experience painful flashbacks and expend enormous amounts of time and energy thinking about our sins and rationalizing our guilt. Physically, we may suffer psychosomatic disorders or a number of illnesses, some of which may result from substance abuse. Relationally, we can alienate ourselves from others. Spiritually, we grieve the Holy Spirit, lose our testimony, and break our fellowship with God. The painful and destructive effects of sin are so profound that why we don't have an aversion to it is a mystery!

Read the first chapter of Jonah. List the results of Jonah's choice of disobedience to God:

In what ways have you seen specific effects of a particular sin in your life?

How can viewing sin as destructive be a motivation for being obedient to God?

Satan is a master of deception and subtlety. He whispers promising suggestions to us. When these thoughts first enter the mind, they hint only at the possibility of forthcoming pleasure, not devastating consequences. While God does allow us to be tempted –

something we have no control over – He has given us His Word and His Spirit so that we can resist Satan and live in obedience to Him.

Read James 4:7-8 and 1 John 4:4. What comforts do you receive from these passages?

What are some ways you can resist Satan's attacks of temptation in the future?

The Father's Discipline

Another purpose of the Holy Spirit is to convict us of sin. Conviction is a form of God's discipline, which serves as proof that we have become sons of God (Heb. 12:5-11). It warns us that we are making choices without regard to either God's truth or sin's consequences. If we choose to be unresponsive to the Holy Spirit, our heavenly Father will discipline us in love. Many people do not understand the difference between discipline and punishment. The following chart shows their profound contrasts:

	PUNISHMENT	DISCIPLINE
SOURCE:	God's Wrath	God's Love
PURPOSE:	To Avenge a Wrong	To Correct a Wrong
RELATIONAL RESULT:	Alienation	Reconciliation
PERSONAL RESULT:	Guilt	A Righteous Lifestyle
DIRECTED TOWARD:	Non-Believers	His Children

Jesus bore all the punishment we deserved on the cross; therefore, we no longer need to fear punishment from God for our sins. We should seek to do what is right so that our Father will not have to correct us through discipline, but when we *are* disciplined, we can remember that God is correcting us in love. His discipline leads us to righteous performance, which is a reflection of the righteousness of Christ.

- Do you sometimes confuse God's correction with punishment? If so, why?

- How can understanding God's discipline be a motivation for you to obey Him?

God's Commands for Us Are Good

God's commands are given for two good purposes: to protect us from the destructiveness of sin, and to direct us in a life of joy and fruitfulness. We have a wrong perspective if we only view God's commands as restrictions in our lives. Instead, we must realize that His commands are guidelines, given so that we might enjoy life to the fullest.

In addition, God's commands are holy, right, and good. Therefore, since they have value in themselves, we should choose to obey God and follow His commands.

Avoid trying to keep God's commands by legalism and self-effort. That leads only to bitterness, condemnation, and rigidity. The Holy Spirit will give you power, joy, and creativity as you trust Him to fulfill the commands of God's Word through you.

Read Rom. 7:12 and 1 John 5:3. How are God's commands described?

Read Deut. 5:29; 6:24. What are some results of obeying God's commands?

How can viewing God's commands as good motivate you to obey them?

Our Obedience Will Be Rewarded

Our self-worth is not based on our performance and obedience; however, what we do (or don't do) has tremendous implications on the quality of our lives and our impact on others for Christ's sake. Disobedience results in spiritual poverty; a short-circuiting of intimate fellowship with the One who loves us so much that He died for us; confusion, guilt, and frustration; and an absence of spiritual power and desire to see people won to Christ and become disciples. On the other hand, responding to the love, grace, and power of Christ enables us to experience His love, joy, and strength as we minister to others, endure difficulties, and live for Him who has ...*called us out of darkness into His marvelous light* (1 Pet. 2:9). We are completely loved, forgiven, and accepted apart from our performance, but how we live is very important!

Read 1 Cor. 3:11-15; 2 Cor. 5:10; 1 John 4:17; and Rev. 20:11-15. According to these passages, *unbelievers* will be judged and condemned at the Great White Throne of Judgment for rejecting Christ. Though *believers* will be spared from this condemnation, we will stand before the Judgment Seat of Christ to have our deeds tested. Deeds done for the Lord will be honored, but deeds done for ourselves will be destroyed by fire. The Greek word to describe this judgment seat is the same word used to describe the platform on which an athlete stands to receive his wreath of victory for winning an event. The Judgment Seat is for the reward of good deeds, not for the punishment of sin.

The following chart demonstrates some of the differences between the Judgment Seat of Christ and the Great White Throne Judgment:

	JUDGMENT SEAT OF CHRIST (1 Cor. 3:11-15)	GREAT WHITE THRONE OF JUDGMENT (Rev. 20:11)
WHO WILL APPEAR:	Christians	Non-Christians
WHAT WILL BE JUDGED:	Deeds	Deeds
PERSONAL RESULT:	Reward	Condemnation
ULTIMATE RESULT:	Used to honor Christ	Cast out of God's presence into the lake of fire

Read 1 Cor. 9:24-27 and 2 Tim. 2:3-7; 4:7-8. How does receiving a reward become a motivation for obedience?

Christ is Worthy

Our most noble motivation for serving Christ is simply that He is worthy of our love and obedience. The Apostle John recorded his vision of the Lord and his response to His glory:

After these things I looked, and behold, a door standing open in heaven, and the first voice which I had heard, like the sound of a trumpet speaking with me, said, "Come up here, and I will show you what must take place after these things."

Immediately I was in the Spirit; and behold, a throne was standing in heaven, and One sitting on the throne.

And He who was sitting was like a jasper stone and a sardius in appearance; and there was a rainbow around the throne, like an emerald in appearance.

And around the throne were twenty-four thrones; and upon the thrones I saw twenty-four elders sitting, clothed in white garments, and golden crown on their heads...

And when the living creatures give glory and honor and thanks to Him who sits on the throne, to Him who lives forever and ever,

the twenty-four elders will fall down before Him who sits on the throne, and will worship Him who lives forever and ever, and will cast their crowns before the throne, saying,

"Worthy art Thou, our Lord and our God, to receive glory and honor and power; for Thou didst create all things, and because of Thy will they existed, and were created."
(Rev. 4:1-4, 9-11)

Each time we choose to obey, we express the righteousness we have in Christ. Our performance, then, becomes a reflection of who we are in Him, and we draw on His power and wisdom so that we can honor Him.

Read 1 Cor. 3:16-17 and 1 Pet. 2:9. How are you described? What purposes for our lives do these passages suggest?

For Additional Reflection and Application
How much are you motivated by each of these six reasons to obey God? Reflect on these motivations and rate each on a scale of zero (no motivation to you at all) to ten (a persistent, conscious, compelling motivation):

_____ The love of Christ motivates us to obey Him.
_____ Sin is destructive.
_____ The Father will discipline us if we continue in a habit of sin.
_____ His commands for us are good.
_____ We will receive rewards for obedience.
_____ Christ is worthy of our obedience.

Do any of these seem "purer" or "higher" to you? If so, which ones? Why?

Which of these do you need to concentrate on? What can you do to further develop this motivation?

Improper Motivations for Obedience

95

Jesus repeatedly emphasized that His concern is not only what we do, but why we do it. The Pharisees obeyed many rules and regulations, but their hearts were far from the Lord. Motives are important! The following represent some poor motivations for obeying God and their possible results:

Someone May Find Out

Many people obey God because they are afraid of what others will think of them if they don't obey. Allen went on church visitation because he feared what his Sunday school class would think if he didn't. Barbara was married, but wanted to go out with a man at work. She didn't because of what others might think.

There are problems with determining behavior solely on the opinions of others. First, there are times when no one is watching. If the motive is to refrain from sin is missing, we may indulge in it. A second problem is that our desire to disobey may eventually exceed the peer pressure to obey. Finally, once someone has found out we've sinned, we may no longer have a reason to obey.

Is the "fear if someone finding out" a motivation for you to obey God? If it is, identify the specific sin you are trying to avoid; then, go back over the six reasons to obey Him. Which of these proper motives seems to encourage you most in regard to your specific sin?

God Will Be Angry with Me

Some people obey God because they think He will get angry with them if they don't. We've already discussed the difference in God's discipline and punishment, but to reiterate, God disciplines us in love, not anger. His response to our sin is grief, not condemnation (Eph. 4:30).

Hank was afraid that God would "zap" him if he did anything wrong, so he performed for God. He lived each day in fear of God's anger. Predictably, his relationship with the Lord was cold and mechanical.

God does not want us to live in fear of His anger, but in response to His love. This produces joyful obedience instead of fear.

If you knew that God's response to your sin was grief instead of anger, would that affect your motivation to obey Him? Why, or why not?

I Couldn't Approve of Myself if I Didn't Obey

Some people obey God in an attempt to live up to certain standards they've set for themselves. Sadly, the idea of yielding their lives to a loving Lord is often far from their minds. They are only trying to live up to their own standards, and if they don't meet those standards, they feel ashamed. These people are primarily concerned with do's and don'ts. Instead of an intimate relationship with God, they see the Christian life as a ritual, with the key emphasis on rules. If these people succeed in keeping the rules, they often become prideful. They may also tend to compare themselves with others, hoping to be accepted on the basis of being a little bit better than someone else.

Phillip was raised in a strict church family. He was taught that cursing is a terrible sin. All of Phillip's friends cursed, but he never did. He secretly thought that he was better than his friends. The issue with Phillip was never what God wanted or God's love for him. Instead, it was his own compulsion to live up to his standards. Phillip needed to base his behavior on God and His Word, not on his own standards.

God gave us His commands out of love for us. We are protected and freed to enjoy life more fully as we obey Him.

What things are you not doing because you couldn't stand yourself if you did them?

What are you doing to obey God with the motivation to meet *your own* standards?

I'll Obey to Be Blessed

God does not swap marbles. If our sole motive to obey is to be blessed, we are simply attempting to manipulate God. The underlying assumption is: *I've been good enough...bless me.* It is true that we will reap what we sow. It is true that obedience keeps us within God's plan for us. But our decision to obey should never be based solely on God's rewarding us.

Brian went to church so that God would bless his business, not because he wanted to worship God. Cheryl chose not to spread gossip about Diane because she told God that she would not tell anybody about Diane if He would get her the promotion she wanted.

Similarly, we may try to bargain with God, saying, *I'll obey You if You will "fix" me.* We reason that if we are "fixed," we will be better equipped to serve God (and we'll be freed from having to deal with a particular problem or temptation). However, God sometimes has something important to teach us through a particular weakness.

The Apostle Paul entreated the Lord three times, asking Him to remove a "thorn," or difficulty, from him. The Lord responded to him: *My grace is sufficient for you, for power is perfected in weakness* (2 Cor. 12:9). Paul concluded: *Most gladly, therefore, I will rather boast about my weaknesses, that the power of Christ may dwell in me. Therefore I am well content with weaknesses, with insults, with distresses, with persecutions, with difficulties, for Christ's sake; for when I am weak, then I am strong* (2 Cor. 12:10).

Do you try to make deals with God? Why, or why not?

How can you apply Paul's words to overcoming chemical dependency?

- To any other situation?

Christ has freed us from the bondage of sin so that we can respond to Him in obedience. We have discussed six biblical reasons to be involved in good works:

1. The love of Christ motivates us to obey Him.
2. Sin is destructive.
3. The Father will discipline us.
4. His commands for us are good.
5. We will receive rewards.
6. Obedience is an opportunity to honor God.

There are times when our feelings seem to get in the way of our obedience. We may want to indulge in some particular sin, or we may be afraid of failure, or what someone might think of us. We may be selfish, or maybe just tired. But the Lord never said pleasant emotions were a prerequisite for following Him. He said, "If anyone wishes to come after Me, let him deny himself (*and the right to pleasant emotions*), and take up his cross daily, and follow Me" (Luke 9:23). This does not mean we should deny our emotions, whether they are positive or negative. We should express them fully to the Lord, telling Him how we feel, and then act in faith on His Word. But spiritual growth, character development, and Christian service should not be held hostage by our emotions. God has given each of us a will, and we can choose to honor the Lord in spite of our feelings.

In different situations, we will draw upon different motivations for obedience. Sometimes, we will need to be reminded of the destructiveness of sin in order to choose righteousness. At other times, we will be truly overwhelmed by God's love and want to honor Him. Either way, it is our underlying motive which determines if our actions are done to honor God or to selfishly make us more acceptable to Him, to others, or ourselves.

Are your emotions prompting you to postpone obedience in any area of your life? If yes, what area(s)?

What steps of action do you need to take to obey the Lord?

As you become more aware of correct motives for obedience, and as you begin to identify improper motivations in your life, you may think, *I've never done anything purely for the Lord in my whole life!* You may feel a sense of pain and remorse for your inappropriate motives. But try not to demean yourself for your past attitudes… they are common to all of us. Instead, realize that the Lord wants you to make godly choices today so that you can enjoy the benefits of those decisions in the future. Then, ask the Holy Spirit to help you develop a sense of intensity about these choices, as Paul wrote, *…we have as our ambition… to be pleasing to Him* (2 Cor. 5:9).

Your motives won't become totally pure until you see the Lord face to face (1 John 3:2), but the more you grow in your understanding of Him and relationship with Him, the more you will desire to honor Him with your love, loyalty, and obedience.

STEP SEVEN

***We humbly ask God to renew our minds so that our sinful patterns can be
transformed into patterns of righteousness.***

*And do not be conformed to this world, but be transformed by the renewing
of your mind, that you may prove what the will of God is,
that which is good and acceptable and perfect. (Rom. 12:2)*

Having examined some pitfalls in our relationship with God, some truths about His
character, the power of His Holy Spirit, and some motivations for obedience, we are now
ready to ask God to reshape us and transform our lives for His glory. The question now
arises, *How do I actually implement His righteousness into my life? How do I continue
the process of change?*

This step is long, but it is crucial. Its perspectives and truths are designed to give you a
solid foundation for a lifetime of spiritual, emotional, and relational health. Remember,
the goal is not to "fill in the blanks," so don't rush through this material. Take time both
to reflect on these truths and apply them deeply to your life.

Renewing Our Minds

Although the Spirit of Christ lives within us and enables us to evaluate our
experiences, our minds tend to dwell on worldly thoughts instead of on God's truth.
Why?

Since the Fall, man's mind has been darkened (Eph. 4:17-19), and he has chosen to
believe the lies of Satan instead of the truths of God's Word. Satan's lies are a direct
result of his character:

*...He (Satan) was a murderer from the beginning, and does not stand in the truth,
because there is no truth in him. Whenever he speaks a lie, he speaks from his nature;
for he is a liar, and the father of lies. (John 8:44)*

Satan's goal is to keep our minds unrenewed so that our lives won't be transformed. He
does this by establishing fortresses of deception, destructive belief systems that are
reinforced over the years by the thoughts, emotions, and actions they produce.

Solomon wrote, *As (a man) thinks within himself, so he is* (Prov. 23:7). Our thoughts
usually affect the way we feel, the way we perceive ourselves and others, and ultimately,
the way we act. The way we think can determine whether we will live according to
God's truth or the world's value system. Writing to the Christians in Rome, Paul
explained the serious implications of how we think:

*And do not be conformed to this world, but be transformed by the renewing of your
mind, that you may prove what the will of God is, that which is good and acceptable and
perfect. (Rom. 12:2)*

Although the way we think often affects the way we feel (and thus, the way we act), it is also true that feelings affect our thoughts and behavior, and that our behavior can affect our feelings and our thinking. In other words, the relationship between thinking, feeling, and acting is not always unidirectional. Our thoughts, emotions, and behaviors are dependent on each other, none exists in a vacuum. However, because beliefs can play a powerful role in shaping our behavior, we will use a model adapted from psychologist Albert Ellis's Rational Emotive Therapy as a starting point for further consideration of their effect on our lives. A simple explanation of this approach is:

Situations

Beliefs ⇒ **Thoughts** ⇒ **Emotions** ⇒ **Actions**

We often interpret the situations we encounter through our beliefs. Some of these interpretations are conscious reflections; most of them, however, are based on unconscious assumptions. These beliefs trigger certain thoughts, which, in turn, stimulate certain emotions, and from these emotions come our actions. In order for an emotion to persist, our belief system must continue to produce certain thoughts. For example, we often will not stay sad without continuing to think sad thoughts. Think of it in this way: Our minds contain deeply held beliefs and attitudes which have been learned through our environment, experiences, and education. These beliefs and attitudes produce thoughts which reflect how we perceive the events in our lives. These thoughts, then, combined with past experiences, relationships, and patterns of behavior, are often the source of our emotions, and our emotions then become the launching pad for our actions.

False Beliefs

If what we believe about ourselves is founded on the truth of God's Word, we are likely to have a positive sense of self-esteem. However, as we mentioned in step 2, Satan has deceived most of mankind by convincing us that:

Our Self-Worth = Performance + Other's Opinions

The four false beliefs we included there serve as a summary of the many lies Satan tells us. These beliefs are listed again below. To what extent are you affected by them? Estimate the percentage which you think indicates how much you live by each belief, from zero to 100 percent:

_____ % *I must meet certain standards in order to feel good about myself.*

_____ % *I must have the approval of certain others (*boss, friends, parents) *to approve of myself.*

If I don't have their approval, I can't feel good about myself.

_____ % *Those who fail are unworthy of love, and deserve to be blamed or condemned.*

_____ % *I am what I am. I cannot change. I am hopeless. In other words, I am the sum total of all my past successes and failures, and I'll never be significantly different.*

The following chart identifies each belief with its consequences, God's specific solution, and the increasing freedom we will gain by living out His solution.

FALSE BELIEFS	CONSEQUENCES OF FALSE BELIEFS	GOD'S SPECIFIC SOLUTION	RESULTS OF GOD'S SOLUTION
I must meet certain standards in order to feel good about myself.	The fear of failure; perfectionism; being driven to succeed; manipulating others to achieve success; withdrawing from healthy risks	Because of *justification,* we are completely forgiven and fully pleasing to God. We no longer have to fear failure.	Increasing freedom from the fear of failure; desire to pursue the right things: Christ and His kingdom; love for Christ
I must have the approval of certain others to feel good about myself.	The fear of rejection; attempting to please others at any cost; being overly sensitive to criticism; withdrawing from others to avoid disapproval	Because of *reconciliation,* we are totally accepted by God. We no longer have to fear rejection.	Increasing freedom from the fear of rejection; willingness to be open and vulnerable; able to relax around others; willingness to take criticism; desire to please God no matter what others think
Those who fail (including me) are unworthy of love and deserve to be punished.	The fear of punishment; propensity to punish others; blaming self and others for personal failure; withdrawing from God and fellow believers; being driven to avoid punishment	Because of *propitiation,* we have the capacity to deeply experience God's love. We no longer have to fear punishment or punish others.	Increasing freedom from the fear of punishment; patience and kindness toward others; being quick to forgive; deep love for Christ
I am what I am, I cannot change. I am hopeless.	Feelings of shame, hopelessness, apathy, inferiority; passivity; loss of creativity; isolation, withdrawing from others	Because of *regeneration,* we have been made brand new, complete in Christ. We no longer need to experience the pain of shame.	Christ-centered self-confidence; joy, courage, peace; desire to know Christ

We will now examine these false beliefs with God's solution for each one:

The Performance Trap

The false belief: *I must meet certain standards in order to feel good about myself,* results in a fear of failure. How affected are you by this belief? Take the following test to determine how strongly you fear failure.

Fear of Failure Test

Read the following statements. Look at the top of the test and choose the term which best describes your response. Put the number above that term in the blank beside each statement.

1	2	3	4	5	6	7
Always	Very Often	Often	Sometimes	Seldom	Very Seldom	Never

_____ 1. Because of fear, I often avoid participating in certain activities.

_____ 2. When I sense I might experience failure in some important area, I become nervous and anxious.

_____ 3. I worry.

_____ 4. I have unexplained anxiety.

_____ 5. I am a perfectionist.

_____ 6. I am compelled to justify my mistakes.

_____ 7. There are certain areas in which I feel I *must* succeed.

_____ 8. I become depressed when I fail.

_____ 9. I become angry with people who interfere with my attempts to succeed, and as a result, make me appear incompetent.

_____ 10. I am self-critical.

_____ Total (Add up the numbers you have placed in the blanks.)

Interpretation of Score

If your score is...

57-70

God has apparently given you a very strong appreciation for His love and unconditional acceptance. You seem to be freed from the fear of failure that plagues most people. (Some people who score this high are either greatly deceived, or have become callous to their emotions as a way to suppress pain.)

47-56

The fear of failure controls your responses rarely, or only in certain situations. Again, the only major exceptions are those who are not honest with themselves.

37-46

When you experience emotional problems, they may relate to a sense of failure or some form of criticism. Upon reflection, you will probably relate many of your previous decisions to this fear. Many of your future decisions will also be affected by the fear of failure unless you take direct action to overcome it.

27-36

The fear of failure forms a general backdrop to your life. There are probably few days that you are not affected in some way by this fear. Unfortunately, this robs you of the joy and peace your salvation is meant to bring.

0-26

Experiences of failure dominate your memory and have probably resulted in a great deal of depression. These problems will remain until some definitive action is taken. In other words, this condition will not simply disappear; time alone cannot heal your pain. You need to experience deep healing in your self-concept, in your relationship with God, and in your relationship with others.

Effects of the Fear of Failure

In the following exercise, we will examine the effects of the fear of failure, which stems from the false belief, *I must meet certain standards in order to feel good about myself.*

List two recent situations in which your performance did not measure up to the standard you had set for yourself. Identify the standard you felt you needed to meet. Then, try to remember what thoughts and emotions accompanied each occasion, and the actions you took that reflected those thoughts and feelings:

Example:

SITUATION: *I failed to make a sale.*
Standards: *I must meet my quota to feel good about myself.*
Thoughts: *I'm a failure. I'll never make my quota. I'll never get promoted. I'll probably be fired any day now.*
Emotions: Fear, anger, depression
Actions: *I avoided my boss for three days. I yelled at my wife and kids, taking out my anger on them.*

Do you see any patterns reflected in your emotions and actions? If so, what are they?

Why do people use performance as a measurement of personal worth?

Do you have to be successful in order to feel good about yourself?

• What would you have to be or do to feel like you are a success?

- In what area(s) would you *never* allow yourself to fail?

Through what roles or activities (including Christian service) are you trying to gain a greater sense of self-worth?

Does performing these activities make you more pleasing to God?

How did your desire to meet certain standards affect your drinking or using habit?

How does your desire to meet your performance standard affect your relationships with others?

How do you feel toward those who hinder your ability to meet your standard?

What do you do to avoid failure?

How do you think your life would be different if you did not experience the fear of failure?

The fear of failure is like stacking marbles – a very difficult task, but not any more difficult than trying to win the performance game. When we evaluate ourselves by our performance, we're ultimately going to lose, no matter how successful we are at the moment.

If we believe that our self-worth is based on our success, we will try to avoid failure at all costs. Most of us have become experts at avoiding failure. We attempt only those things in which we are confident of success. We avoid those activities where the risk of failure is too great. We spend time around those who are not a threat to us. We avoid people who, either by their greater success or by their disapproval of us, make us feel like failures. We have trained ourselves very well!

Another consequence of having to *meet certain standards in order to feel good about ourselves* is a rules-dominated life. Many of us know people who have a set of rules for everything, and who always place their attention on their performance. However, the focus of the gospel is on relationships, not regulations. Christ's exercise of His lordship in our lives is dependent on our attending to His moment-by-moment instruction. Focusing only on rules will relegate our lives to the prison of self-examination.

On the other hand, we may be feeling very good about ourselves because we are winning the performance game. We may be so talented that we are reaching virtually every goal we have set for ourselves. We can't afford to mistake this pride for positive

104

self-worth. We must realize that God is able to bring about whatever circumstances are necessary to cause us to stop trusting in ourselves, God intends to bring us to Himself through prayer and the study of His Word so that we can know, love, and serve Him. Sometimes, He will allow us to fail miserably so that we will look to Him instead of to ourselves for our security and significance. Before becoming upset that God would allow you to experience failure, remember that any life less than God intended is a second-class existence. He loves you too much to let you continue to obtain your self-esteem from the empty promise of success.

God's Answer: Justification

As a result of Christ's death of the cross, our sins are forgiven and God has imputed Christ's righteousness to us. We have been *justified* by Christ. Therefore, we are fully pleasing to God.

Read Rom. 3:19-28; 4:4-5; 5:1-11. What does it mean to be *justified?*

Read 2 Cor. 5:21; Col. 1:22; 3:12; and Heb. 10:14. Are you as righteous, holy, and blameless as Christ: Why, or why not?

Read Rom. 3:9-23; 5:6-10; and Eph. 2:1-3. Why did you need to be justified and have Christ's righteousness attributed to you? Describe God's view of you before your justification:

How was you justification accomplished?

- Rom. 3:24; Titus 3:7
- Rom. 3:28; Gal. 2:16
- Rom. 5:1; Gal 3:24
- Rom. 5:9; Heb. 9:22

What are the results of justification?

- Rom. 4:7-8
- Rom. 5:1

- Rom. 5:9
- Rom. 8:1,33-34
- 2 Cor. 5:14-15
- 2 Cor. 5:21
- Titus 3:7

Read Rom. 4:6-8 and Heb. 10:17. Are you remembering sins that God has forgotten? If so, why?

- Does remembering sin help you in any way? If so, how?

How does being justified and having Christ's righteousness lead you to the conclusion: *I am completely forgiven by God, and am fully pleasing to Him?*

If your good works won't make you more pleasing to God, why should you be involved in good works? (See Rom. 6:12-13; 1 Cor. 6:18-20; Col. 3:23-24; and Titus 2:11-14.)

Read 1 Cor. 3:11-16. What will determine whether or not a deed will honor God? (See also Rom. 14:23 and 1 Cor. 10:31.)

Review the "situations" you described previously in this step. Using one of the occasions you listed, chart how your behavior would have been different if you had believed the truth that you are completely forgiven by God, and are fully pleasing to Him, rather than the false belief, *I must meet certain standards in order to feel good about myself.*

Example:

- SITUATION:
- Belief: *I am completely forgiven and fully pleasing to God.*
- Thoughts:
- Emotions:
- Actions:

Memorize Rom. 5:1.

If we base our self-worth on our ability to meet standards, we will try to compensate, either by avoiding risks or by trying to succeed no matter what the cost. Either way, failure looms as a constant enemy. But God has a solution for the fear of failure! He has given us a secure self-worth totally apart from our ability to perform. We have been justified, placed in right standing before God through Christ's death on the cross, which paid for our sins. But God didn't stop with forgiving us; He also granted us the very righteousness of Christ!

Visualize two ledgers: on one is a list of all your sins; on the other, a list of the righteousness of Christ. Now exchange your ledger for Christ's. This exemplifies justification – transferring our sin to Christ and His righteousness to us. In 2 Cor. 5:21, Paul wrote: *He made Him* (Christ) *who knew no sin to be sin on our behalf, that we might become the righteousness of God in Him.*

Justification carries no guilt with it, and has no memory of past transgressions. Christ paid for all our sins at the cross – past, present, and future. Hebrews 10:17 says, *And their sins and their lawless deeds I will remember no more.* We are completely forgiven by God! In the same act of love through which God forgave our sin, He also provided for our *righteousness:* the worthiness to stand in His presence.

By imputing righteousness to us, God attributes Christ's worth to us. The moment we accept Christ, God no longer sees us as condemned sinners. Instead, we are forgiven, we receive Christ's righteousness, and God sees us as creatures who are fully pleasing to Him.

God intended that Adam and his descendants be righteous people, fully experiencing His love and eternal purposes. But sin short-circuited that relationship. God's perfect payment for sin has since satisfied His righteous wrath, enabling us again to have that status of righteousness, and to delight in knowing and honoring the Lord.

God desires for those of us who have been redeemed to experience the realities of His redemption. We are forgiven and righteous because of Christ's sacrifice; therefore, we are pleasing to God in spite of our failures. This reality can replace our fear of failure with peace, hope, and joy. Failure need not be a millstone around our necks. Neither success nor failure is the proper basis of our self-worth. Christ alone is the source of our forgiveness, freedom, joy, and purpose.

Approval Addict

Living by the false belief: *I must be approved by certain others to feel good about myself,* causes us to continually fear rejection, and conform virtually all of our attitudes and actions to the expectations of others. How are you affected by this belief? Take the following test to determine how strongly you fear rejection.

Fear of Rejection Test

Read the following statements. Look at the top of the test and choose the term which best describes your response. Put the number above that term in the blank beside each statement.

1	2	3	4	5	6	7
Always	Very Often	Often	Sometimes	Seldom	Very Seldom	Never

_____ 1. I avoid certain people.

_____ 2. When I sense that someone might reject me, I become nervous and anxious.

_____ 3. It bothers me when someone is unfriendly to me.

_____ 4. I am uncomfortable around those who are different from me.

_____ 5. I am basically shy and unsocial.

_____ 6. I am critical of others.

_____ 7. I find myself trying to impress others.

_____ 8. I become depressed when someone criticizes me.

_____ 9. I always try to determine what people think of me.

_____ 10. I don't understand people and what motivates them.

_____ Total (Add up the numbers you have placed in the blanks.)

Interpretation of Score

If your score is...

57-70

God has apparently given you a very strong appreciation for His love and unconditional acceptance. You seem to be freed from the fear of rejection that plagues most people. (Some people who score this high are either greatly deceived, or have become callous to their emotions as a way to suppress pain.)

47-56

The fear of rejection controls your responses rarely, or only in certain situations. Again, the only major exceptions are those who are not honest with themselves.

37-46

When you experience emotional problems, they may relate to a sense of rejection. Upon reflection, you will probably relate many of your previous decisions to this fear. Many of your future decisions will also be affected by the fear of rejections unless you take direct action to overcome it.

27-36

The fear of rejection forms a general backdrop to your life. There are probably few days that you are not in some way affected by this fear. Unfortunately, this robs you of the joy and peace your salvation is meant to bring.

0-26

Experiences of rejection dominate your memory and have probably resulted in a great deal of depression. These problems will persist until some definitive action is taken. In other words, this condition will not simply disappear; time alone cannot heal your pain. You need to experience deep healing in your self-concept, in your relationship with God, and in your relationships with others.

Effects of the Fear of Rejection

The following exercise is designed to help you understand the fear of rejection and the resulting false belief, *I must be approved by certain others to feel good about myself.*

Are you adversely affected by anyone's disrespect or disapproval? If so, list those individuals or groups:

To see how others' expectations can affect you, select one of the many people in the first question and answer the following:

* _____ would be more pleased with me if I would:

a)
b)
c)

* _____ is proud of me when I:

a)
b)
c)

* How does _____ attempt to get me to change by what he or she says and does?

a)
b)
c)

* Things I do or say to get _____ to approve of me include:

a)
b)
c)

(Use a separate sheet of paper for each of the people or groups you just listed.)
List several specific instances when others (friends, boss, parents) have withheld approval, or have used criticism, silence, or sarcasm to manipulate you into doing what they wanted you to do. What did they say or do? Did they succeed? Why, or why not?

What belief is rooted in the fear of disapproval?

How has the fear of rejection influenced your moral standards (drinking, drug abuse, theft, lying, sexual behavior, lifestyle, etc.)? Can you recall specific instances in your life when this fear has greatly influenced your morals? If so, list them. How did the fear of rejection affect your behavior?

If you run from rejection, who is really in control of your life?

How have you used disapproval, silence, sarcasm, or criticism to get others to do what you wanted them to do?

How did you use alcohol or drugs to get others to do what you wanted them to do?

Sometimes, rather than praising others because we genuinely appreciate them, we use praise as a form of manipulation. Our motive is to influence them to do something we want them to do.

• How do you feel when people praise you only to manipulate you?

• Have you used praise to manipulate others? If so, why, and how have you used it?

• How could manipulating others by praising them be considered a form of rejection?

For whatever reason and or whatever degree we have experienced rejection, our fear of going through that pain again can affect us profoundly. We learn how to deal with physical injury early in life, but because emotional pain is sometimes perceived as a sign of weakness, and because we have not learned how to respond appropriately to this pain, we avoid it. If we are hurt, we may attempt to deny our pain by ignoring it. We may drive ourselves to accomplish tasks which we think others will approve of. Some of us can't say no for this reason. Or, we may become passive, withdrawing from others and avoiding those decisions and activities which others might criticize, or which can't guarantee success for us. Our goal in these instances is usually to avoid the pain of rejection by not doing anything which might be objectionable, but this also prevents us from enjoying the pleasures of healthy relationships and achievements.

Other behaviors related to the fear of rejection include:

1. being easily manipulated
2. being hypersensitive to criticism
3. defensiveness

4. hostility toward others who disagree with us
5. superficial relationships
6. exaggerating or minimizing the truth to impress people
7. shyness
8. passivity
9. nervous breakdown

Evaluating our self-worth by what we and others think of our performance leads us to believe that any time our performance is unacceptable, we are unacceptable as well. To some extent, virtually all of us have internalized the following sentence into our belief system, and hold to it with amazing tenacity: *I must have acceptance, respect, and approval in order to have self-worth.* This is the basic false belief behind all peer pressure.

Rejection can be communicated in a number of ways. We can easily see how criticism, sarcasm, and silence convey this message, but it may not be quite so obvious that praise can also serve as a form of manipulation and is, therefore, a form of rejection. We must ask ourselves what we are trying to accomplish when we praise someone. What is our goal? If we desire to help the person, to build him or her up, and to instill encouragement through appreciation, then praise is a godly form of communication. If, however, our desire is to get someone else to assist in accomplishing our goals, to contribute to our program, or to help us look good in front of others, then praise is a subtle but powerful form of rejection. Unfortunately, many people – including us – fall prey to this manipulative praise because we so desperately want to be appreciated, and will often do whatever it takes to get it from others.

If you realize that you manipulate others through praise, confess it as sin, and choose to seek their good instead of your goal. Be willing to ask, *What am I trying to accomplish?* in your interaction with others, and strive to communicate genuine, heartfelt appreciation because Christ has given them worth by sacrificing His life for them.

There are four basic levels of acceptance and rejection. Understanding these will help you understand the nature of your relationships with other people, concerning both how you are treated and how you treat them. These levels center around the question: *What does one have to do to be accepted?* These levels are:

1. *Total Rejection:* "No matter what you do, it is not good enough." Example: relationships characterized by deep bitterness or hurt.
2. *Highly Conditional Acceptance:* "You must meet certain requirements to be accepted." Examples: most jobs, relationships with demanding people.
3. *Mildly Conditional Acceptance:* "I will be more happy with you if you do these things." Examples: most marriages, most parent-child relationships, most friendships.
4. *Unconditional Acceptance;* " I love you and accept you no matter what you do. There is nothing you can do that can make me stop loving you." (This does not mean that we can do as we please or that we are to ignore unacceptable behavior in others. Unconditional acceptance may include loving confrontation, correction, and, in some cases, discipline. The focus here is on the individual rather than his or her behavior.) Examples: God, and typically, relationships in which one person's needs are not dependent on the other's.

Make a list of the major relationships in your life: family members, friends, people in your school, office, church, etc. How does each of these people tend to treat you? How do you tend to treat each of them? How should you respond to each of them? How can you put fewer demands and conditions on your acceptance of them?

God's Answer: Reconciliation

God's answer to the pain of rejection is reconciliation. Christ died for our sins and restored us to a proper relationship with God. We are both acceptable to Him and accepted by Him. We are not rejected! We are His.

Define *reconcile.* (Use a dictionary if necessary).

- Who caused the alienation in your relationship with God (Is. 53:6; 59:2; Rom. 3:9-12)?

Read Eph. 2:1-3 and 2 Thess. 1:8-9. How severe was the barrier between you and Holy God?

Read Col 1:21-22. Compare your former state to your present condition in Christ:

Read Rom. 5:8-11. Who initiated restoring your relationship with God?

- How did God reconcile you to Himself?

- What is your response to God? (What does it mean to *exult?)*

What is wrong with the statement, *Thank You, Lord, for accepting me even though I am so unacceptable?*

- Are you currently acceptable?

- To what degree are you acceptable?

- To whom are you acceptable?

- Why are you acceptable?
If you are completely and fully accepted by the perfect Creator of the universe, why is it still so painful to be rejected by other people?

Read John 17:19-26 and 20:17 to see the extent of your reconciliation to God.

- Whom does the Father love more: Jesus Christ or you?

- How does Christ refer to you in John 20:17?

- How do these verses make you feel?

Can you think of two recent situations in which you felt rejected, or in which someone disapproved of something you said or did? If so, list them. Describe your response. How would your response have been different if you had believed the truth of your total acceptance in Christ?

- SITUATION:
- Your Response:
- How Believing the Truth Would Have Changed Your Response:

- SITUATION:
- Your Response:
- How Believing the Truth Would Have Changed Your Response:

Memorize Col. 1:21-22.

When God chose to redeem us so that we could relate to Him and rule with Him, He did not go part way. He did not make us partially righteous, nor has He allowed for our righteousness to be marred by poor performance. The blood of Christ is sufficient to pay for all sin. Because of His blood, we are holy and righteous before God, even in the midst of sin. This does not minimize the inherent destructiveness of sin, but it glorifies the indescribable sacrifice of Christ.

There is no biblical tenet more neglected in its practical application than the doctrine of reconciliation. The Colossian reference to this doctrine reveals its application to us:

And although you were formerly alienated and hostile in your mind, engaged in evil deeds,
yet He has now reconciled you in His fleshly boldly through death, in order to present you before Him holy and blameless and beyond reproach...(Col. 1:21-22)

Relish those last words. God sees us as *holy and blameless and beyond reproach* at this very moment. This is not merely a reference to our future standing; it describes our present status as well. We are totally accepted by God.

God received us into a loving, intimate, personal relationship the moment we placed our faith in Christ. We are united with God in an eternal and inseparable bond (Rom. 8:38-39). We are born of God in an indissoluble union as fellow heirs with Christ. Recognizing that no sin can make a Christian unacceptable to God is God-honoring faith in a blood-sealed warrant with the Holy Spirit, *who is given as a pledge of our inheritance, with a view to the redemption of God's own possession...* (Eph. 1:14).

Since our relationship with God was bought entirely by the blood of Christ, no amount of good works can make us more acceptable to Him. Titus 3:5 says: *He saved us, not on the basis of deed which we have done in righteousness, but according to His mercy...* Because Christ has reconciled us to God, we can experience the incredible truth, *We are totally accepted by and acceptable to God.*

What should we do when we have failed or when someone disapproves of us? A practical way of summarizing the truth we've examined is:

It would be nice if _____ (my boss liked me, I could fix the refrigerator, my complexion were clear, James had picked me up on time, or...) but I'm still deeply loved, completely forgive, fully pleasing, totally accepted, and complete in Christ.

This statement doesn't mean that we won't feel pain or anger. We need to be honest about our feelings. A statement like the one above is simply a quick way to gain God's perspective on whatever we are experiencing. It is not magic, but it enables us to reflect on the implications of biblical truth. We can apply this truth in every difficult situation, whether it involves someone's disapproval, our own failure to accomplish something, or the failure of another person. Memorize the truth in the above statement and begin to apply it in your situations and relationships.

The Blame Game

This false belief: *Those who fail (including myself) are unworthy of love and deserve to be punished,* is at the root of our fear of punishment and propensity to punish others. How deeply are you affected by this lie? Take the test on the next page to determine how much it influences your life.

Fear of Punishment/Punishing Others Test

Read the following statements. Look at the top of the test and choose the term which best describes your response. Put the numbers above that term in the blank beside each statement.

1	2	3	4	5	6	7
Always	Very Often	Often	Sometimes	Seldom	Very Seldom	Never

_____ 1. I fear what God might do to me.

_____ 2. After I fail, I worry about God's response.

_____ 3. When I see someone in a difficult situation, I wonder what he or she did to deserve it.

_____ 4. When something goes wrong, I have a tendency to think that God must be punishing me.

_____ 5. I am very hard on myself when I fail.

_____ 6. I find myself wanting to blame others when they fail.

_____ 7. I get angry with God when someone who is immoral or dishonest prospers.

_____ 8. I am compelled to tell others when I see them doing wrong.

_____ 9. I tend to focus on the faults and failures of others.

_____10.God seems harsh to me.

_____ Total (Add up the numbers you have placed in the blanks.)

Interpretation of Score
If your score is...

57-50
God apparently has given you a very strong appreciation for His unconditional love and acceptance. You seem to be freed from the fear of punishment that plagues most people. (Some people who score this high are either greatly deceived, or have become callous to their emotions as a way to suppress pain.)

47-56
The fear of punishment and the compulsion to punish others control your responses rarely or only in certain situations. Again, the only exceptions are those who are not honest with themselves.

37-46
When you experience emotional problems, they may tend to relate to a fear of punishment or to an inner urge to punish others. Upon reflection, you will probably relate many of your previous decisions to this fear. Many of your future decisions will also be affected by the fear of punishment and/or the compulsion to punish others unless you take direct action to overcome this tendency.

27-36
The fear of punishment forms a general backdrop to your life. There are probably few days that you are not affected in some way by the fear of punishment and the propensity to blame others. Unfortunately, this robs you of the joy and peace your salvation is meant to bring.

0-26
Experiences of punishment dominate your memory, and you probably have experienced a great deal of depression. These problems will remain until some definitive plan is followed. In other words, this condition will not simply disappear, time alone cannot heal your pain. You need to experience deep healing in your self-concept, in your relationship with God, and in your relationships with others.

Effects of the Fear of Punishment and Propensity to Punish Others
The exercise will help you understand the fear of punishment and the false belief, *Those who fail are unworthy of love and deserve to be blamed and condemned.*

Do you really deserve to feel good about yourself? Why, or why not?

Describe three recent incidents in your life in which you feared being blamed or punished. What prompted this fear?

Do you spend much time thinking about your weaknesses and failures? If so, why? (List as many reasons as you can.)

- What are the three most negative terms you use to describe yourself? What derogatory names do you call yourself?

Does condemning yourself help you to be a better person? Why, or why not?

Think of a close friend or family member with whom you've had a conflict.

- What did you say or do to inflict emotional pain?

- What are some reasons you said or did those things?

After sinning, do you ever believe you have to feel badly about yourself before you can feel good about yourself? If so, list some of the situations in which you've done this:

Do you want to go to the Father after you've sinned? Why, or why not?

If something goes wrong, do you assume the Lord is punishing you?

Does God punish His children?

The proof of blame's effectiveness is that we use it so often. We often believe that we deserve to be blamed for any significant shortcoming, and think self-inflicted punishment will clear us of guilt and enable us to feel good about ourselves again. Why?

We have been conditioned to accept personal blame or condemnation every time our performance is unsatisfactory. After reading, this, some people immediately recognize this automatic response in their lives, but others do not. You may think that you are not affected by this false belief at all – but you probably are. Do you generally have an urge to find out who is at fault when something fails? Do you look for excuses when you fail?

Rather than evaluating our problems objectively, most of us tend to defend ourselves. Counterattack triggers counterattack. The more we criticize other people, the more defensive they usually get, and the less likely they are to admit their errors (especially to us). Criticism can lead to a counterattack from both sides, and pretty soon, it is like a volleyball game, with each person intensifying the pace while returning blame to the other person's side.

116

However, it is sometimes even more destructive for people to accept blame without defending themselves. Tom was becoming an emotional zombie under his wife's incessant condemnation, but instead of fighting back, he kept thinking, *Yes, Suzanne's right. I am an incompetent fool.* He was like the worn-out punching bag of a heavyweight fighter.

Both self-inflicted punishment and the compulsion to punish others result from the false belief: Those *who fail are unworthy of love and deserve to be blamed and condemned.*

God's Answer: Propitiation

At the cross, God poured out His wrath against sin. This exercise will help you see that God's wrath has been satisfied; therefore, we have no need to fear punishment.

Define *propitiation.* (Use a dictionary if necessary).

We each have had an incalculable number of sinful (disobedient, self-centered) thoughts and actions. How many sins can a Holy God overlook?

Read Ezek. 7:8-9; Rom. 2:4-5; and Eph. 2:1-3. Does God's wrath have a specific object? If so, what is it?

Read Gen. 19:1-26; Jer. 4:4; Ezek. 5:11-17; 23:22-30; and 2 Thess. 1:6-10. List some characteristics of God's wrath from these passages:

Read 1 John 4:9-10.

- Are you loved by the Father?

- How do you know you are loved?

- Do you feel loved?
Consider what it would be like to experience the wrath of Almighty God, and then read Is. 53:4-10. Place your name in the place of appropriate pronouns ("Surely he took up _____'s infirmities.") The wrath that you deserved has been poured out on Christ.

- In what ways can you express gratitude to Christ for what He has done for you?

The more we understand God's love and forgiveness, the more we will be willing and able to forgive others. If we think about it, the things that others do to us are all trivial in comparison to our sin of rebellion against God that He has graciously forgiven. This is why Paul encouraged the Colossian Christians to forgive each other *just as God in Christ also has forgiven you* (Eph. 4:32), completely and willingly.

- Are there any sins (or even personality differences) in others that you have difficulty forgiving? If so, list them and confess to God your lack of forgiveness:

- How do these compare to your sins that deserved God's wrath, but received the payment of Christ's substitutionary death?

Memorize 1 John 4:9-10.

God's plan for us is centered in the cross. To understand His plan, we must first understand the meaning of propitiation.

Prior to our spiritual birth, even our good deeds were despicable to God (Is. 64:6). If we are honest about our performance, we must admit that we have sinned thousands of times, even after having accepted Christ.

The problem with our sinfulness is that God is absolutely holy, pure, and perfect. There is absolutely nothing unholy in Him. *God is light, and in Him there is no darkness at all* (1 John 1:5). Therefore, since God is holy, He cannot overlook or compromise with sin. It took one sin to separate Adam from God. For God to condone even *one* sin would instantly defile His holiness, which He indicates by His righteous condemnation of sin (Rom. 6:23).

The Father did not escape witnessing His Son's mistreatment: the mocking, the scourging, and the cross. He could have spoken and ended the whole ordeal, yet He kept silent. Confronted with the suffering of His Son, He chose to let it continue so that we could be saved. What an expression of love! Its depth is unsearchable.

Try to recall an experience in which you felt loved by someone else. That person cared about you and wanted to be with you. You didn't have to perform; just being you was enough. The thought of that person selecting you to love was intoxicating. All other facets of life seemed to diminish. He or she loved you, and that love was soothing to you and satisfied many of your inner longings.

If the love of a person can make us feel this way, consider how much greater joy the heavenly Father's love can bring. We can't truly appreciate the Father's love unless we realize that it supersedes any experience of being loved by another man or woman.

God loves you, and He enjoys revealing His love to you. He enjoys being loved by you, but He knows you can love Him only if you are experiencing His love for you. Propitiation means that His wrath has been removed and that you are deeply loved!

Many of us have a distorted concept of the heavenly Father. We believe that God is thrilled when we accept Christ and are born into His family. But many of us also believe that He is proud of us for only as long as we perform well, and that the better our performance, the happier He is with us.

In reality, God loves us, and not a moment goes by that He isn't thinking loving thoughts about us (Ps. 40:5). We are His children and we individually special to Him because of Christ! Propitiation, then, means that Jesus Christ has satisfied the Father's righteous condemnation of sin by His death. The Scriptures give only one reason to explain this incredible fact: God loves you!

118

Shame

When we base our self-worth on past failures, dissatisfaction with personal appearance, or bad habits, we often develop a fourth false belief: *I am what I am. I cannot change. I am hopeless.* This lie binds people to the hopeless pessimism associated with poor self-esteem. Take the following test to establish how strongly you experience shame.

Shame Test

Read the statements below. Look at the top of the test and choose the term which best describes your response. Put the number above that term in the blank beside each statement.

1	2	3	4	5	6	7
Always	Very Often	Often	Sometimes	Seldom	Very Seldom	Never

_____ 1. I often think about past failures or experiences of rejection.

_____ 2. There are certain things about my past which I cannot recall without xperiencing strong, painful emotions (i.e., guilt, shame, anger, fear, etc.)

_____ 3. I seem to make the same mistakes over and over again.

_____ 4. There are certain aspects of my character I want to change, but I don't believe I an ever successfully do so.

_____ 5. I feel inferior.

_____ 6. There are aspects of my appearance that I cannot accept.

_____ 7. I am generally disgusted with myself.

_____ 8. I feel that certain experiences have basically ruined my life.

_____ 9. I perceive of myself as an immoral person.

_____ 10. I feel I have lost the opportunity to experience a complete and wonderful life.

_____ Total (Add up the numbers you have placed in the blanks.)

Interpretation of Score

If your score is...

57-70

God has apparently given you a very strong appreciation for His love and unconditional acceptance. You seem to be freed from the shame that plagues most people. (Some people who score this high are either greatly deceived, or have become callous to their emotions as a way to suppress pain.)

47-56

Shame controls your responses rarely or only in certain situations. Again, the exceptions are those who are not honest with themselves.

37-46

When you experience emotional problems, they may relate to a sense of shame. Upon reflection, you will probably relate many of your previous decisions to a poor sense of self-worth. Many of your future decisions will also be affected by low self-esteem unless you take direct action to overcome it.

27-36

Shame forms a generally negative backdrop to your life. There are probably few days in which you are not affected in some way by shame. Unfortunately, this robs you of the joy and peace your salvation was meant to bring.

0-26

Experiences of shame dominate your memory, and have probably resulted in a great deal of depression. These problems will remain until some definitive action is taken. In other words, this condition will not simply disappear one day; time alone cannot heal your pain. You must deal with its root issue.

Effects of Shame

This exercise examines the shame that can arise from a negative evaluation of our past performance and/or physical appearance. Shame leads to the false belief: *I am what I am. I cannot change. I am hopeless.*

Define *shame:*

When do you experience shame?

In what ways does shame make an impact on our sense of self-worth? How does shame lock us into a low opinion of ourselves?

Is there anything you can't keep from doing? When you've tried to stop but then do it again, how do you feel about yourself?

List aspects of your appearance or past performance which prevent you from viewing yourself as a fully pleasing and totally accepted person:

- Appearance:
- Past Performance:

When people with a poor self-concept succeed at something, one would think that they would be encouraged and have a more positive outlook. But often, pessimistic people explain or minimize their success and continue in their hopelessness.

- Do you do this when you succeed?

- If so, what do you tell yourself and others?

- Why do you say those things?

What sources of input reinforce this low view of yourself?

Read Ps. 139:13-16. What was God's involvement in the formation of your physical appearance and personality?

If you have a poor self-concept, what do you think it will take to overcome it and experience the joy and power of your new life in Christ?

How do you think other people would describe you?

- What are their expectations of you?

- How have their expectations affected your self-esteem?

Shame often results from instances of neglect or abuse, and is then reinforced by failures in our performance or "flaws" in our appearance. Even when others don't know of our failure, we assume their opinion of us is poor and adopt what we think their opinion might be.

If we base our self-worth on our performance long enough, our past behavior will eventually become the sole basis of our worth. We will see ourselves with certain character qualities and flaws because that's the way we have always been. We then have unconsciously incorporated Satan's lie into our belief system: *I must always be what I have been, and live with whatever self-worth I have, because that's just me.* Interestingly, we claim only our *poor* behavior as *That's just me.* We never hear anyone saying, "That's just me. I'm so wonderful, honest, and bright."

We may think that humility is self-depreciation, but true humility is an accurate appraisal of our worth in Christ: We deserved God's righteous condemnation, yet we are recipients of His unconditional love, grace, and righteousness through Christ. We are deeply loved, completely forgiven, fully pleasing, totally accepted, and complete in Him. Thankfulness, generosity, kindness, and self-confidence constitute true humility!

Another aspect of a poor self-concept relates to personal appearance. Most of us have some aspect of our appearance that we wish we could change, but much about our appearance can't really be altered. We may not only base our self-worth on our appearance, but may tend to base our acceptance of others on their appearance, even the color of their skin. We may never be any more cruel than when we accept or reject others based on their appearance.

Are you angry with God for the way He made you? Do you compare and rank you appearance with that of others? If you do, you will suffer at some point in your life because there will always be someone prettier, stronger, cuter, or more handsome. Even if you are spectacularly beautiful or strikingly handsome, you will suffer because you will be afraid of losing your good looks, the basis of self-worth.

If we insist on valuing our worth by our appearance and performance, sooner or later God will graciously allow us to see the futility of that struggle. God created our need for a sense of significance. However, He knows we will never come to Him until we find the importance of people's opinions to be empty and hopeless. At that point, we can turn to Him and find comfort and encouragement in the truths of His Word.

God's Answer: Regeneration

This exercise will help you see yourself as a new creature in Christ, with new potential and new capacities. The truth that you have been made new in Christ will enable you to develop a strong, positive self-esteem in spite of "flaws " in your appearance or past failures.

? Do you really think that you can view yourself any differently than you always have? If not, why?

Read 2 Cor. 5:17.

- Define *regeneration:*

- What does your having been made a *new creature* mean to you?

How was your regeneration accomplished?

- John 1:12-13
- John 3:16
- Titus 3:5
- 1 Pet. 1:3
- 1 Pet. 1:23

Read Eph. 4:22-24 and Col. 3:9-10. What process do you need to complete in order to experience your new self?

List characteristics of your old and new self based on the passages given here.

Example:

CHARACTERISTICS OF MY OLD SELF	CHARACTERISTICS OF MY NEW SELF
Gal. 5:19-21	Rom. 8:16-17

Eph. 4:17-22	2 Cor. 5:21
Col. 3:5-9	Gal 5:22-23
Titus 3:3	Eph. 4:23-32
	Col 2:10
	Col. 3:10-15
	1 Pet. 1:16

Read Rom. 6:12-23 and 1 Cor. 6:9-11. How does the truth of regeneration free you from evaluating yourself by your past performance?

Read 1 Sam. 16:6-7 and Ps. 139:13-16. How does the truth of regeneration free you from the shame of flaws in your physical appearance?

How could understanding your newness in Christ affect your personal fitness or grooming habits?

How can knowing that you have a new life in Christ affect the way you think, feel, and act?

Do you use past failures, your appearance, or some other "flaw" as an excuse for not living for Christ? If so, what is your excuse? How valid is it?

Memorize 2 or. 5:17.

Regeneration is the renewing work of the Holy Spirit by which a person literally becomes a new creation. Our regeneration occurred at the instant of our conversion to

Christ. At that moment, we were given more than a change of direction; we received the impartation of new life.

The part of us that the Holy Spirit regenerated is our spirit. The Holy Spirit has energized our inner spirit with new life. Jesus called it a new birth in John 3:3, 5-6, saying, "That which is born of the flesh is flesh, and that which is born of the Spirit is spirit" (John 3:6). Regeneration is the Spirit-wrought renewal of our human spirit, a transforming resuscitation so that *the spirit is alive* within us (Rom. 8:10).

The Holy Spirit has been joined to our human spirit, forming a new spiritual entity. A new birth has produced a new being. *Therefore, if any man is in Christ, he is a new creature; the old things passed away; behold, new things have come* (2 Cor. 5:17).

Study these words carefully. Ephesians 4:24 says that our new self *has* (already) *been created in righteousness and holiness of the truth,* but we must yet *put* on this new self in order to progressively produce godly thoughts and actions – as the acorn produces an oak tree!

What is the basis of your self-worth? Are you living by scriptural truths or by false beliefs? False beliefs are all a part of Satan's insidious plan. By now, you may see deception as a part of his scheme to steal, and kill, and destroy mankind. In order to prevent him from victimizing us with lies, it will be helpful not only to recognize and reject them, but to replace them with the truth of God's Word.

The following exercises provide some steps we can take to reject Satan's lies and replace them with a stronghold of truth in our minds.

Making a Truth Card

A simple 3x5 card can be a key factor in helping you base your self-worth on the liberating truths of the Scriptures.

- On the front, write out both the following truths and their corresponding verses from Scripture. On the back of the card, write out the four false beliefs.

Scriptural Truths	False Beliefs
I am completely forgiven and am fully pleasing to God (Rom. 5:1)	*I must meet certain standards in order to feel good about myself.*
I am totally accepted by God (Col. 1:21-22).	*I must be accepted by certain people in order to feel good about myself.*
I am deeply loved by God (1 John 4:9-10).	*Those who fail are unworthy of love and deserve to be blamed and condemned.*
I am a new creation- complete in Christ (2 Cor. 5:17)	*I am what I am. I cannot change. I am hopeless.*

Carry this card with you continuously. Each time you are about to do a routine activity, like having something to drink, look at the front side and slowly meditate on each phrase. Thank the Lord for making you into a person who has these qualities. By

124

doing this for the next twenty-eight days, you will develop a habit of remembering that you are *deeply loved, completely forgiven, fully pleasing, totally accepted, and complete in Christ.*

If you have not already done so, memorize the supporting verses listed on the card over the next four days. Look in your Bible for other verses that support these truths and commit them to memory. Doing this will establish God's Word as the basis for these truths (Col. 3:16). Also memorize the false beliefs. The more familiar you are with these lies, the more you will be able to recognize them in your thoughts. Then, as you recognize them, you can more readily replace them with the truths of God's Word.

Exposing Ungodly Thoughts

Our thoughts reveal what we really believe, yet it is difficult for most of us to be objective in our thinking simply because we haven't trained ourselves to be. We usually let any and every though run its course in our minds without analyzing its worth. Is it a God-honoring thought, or is it a *speculation,* or a *lofty thing raised up against the knowledge of God?* (2 Cor. 10:5).

As we grow in our knowledge of God's Word, we will increasingly be able to identify thoughts that reflect Satan's deceptions. Then, we can reject those lies and replace them with scriptural truth, just as our Lord did when He was tempted by Satan in the wilderness (Matt. 4:1-11). One way of identifying deceptive thoughts is to state what is true and see what comes to mind. Hopefully, our thoughts will increasingly reflect our thankfulness to God for who He is and what He has done for us, but sometimes we will respond by contradicti ng the truth.

For example, you might respond to the truth that you are fully pleasing to God by thinking, *No, I'm not! I mess up all the time, and to be fully pleasing, I'd have to be perfect!* When we see it written out, we more easily recognize that response as a lie. However, we seldom write down our thoughts and analyze their validity.

As a first step in this analysis, write down your thoughts in response to the four truths we've examined. (Again, they will probably be mixed: some positive, thankful, and godly, and some contradictory to the truth.)

- *I am deeply loved by God:*

- *I am completely forgiven and fully pleasing to God:*

- *I am totally accepted by God:*

- *I am complete in Christ:*

Thoughts that contradict these truths are lies. Reject them and replace them with passages of Scripture to reinforce the truth in your mind. Here are some passages to reflect on:

Propitiation: Matt. 18:21-35; Luke 7:36-50; Rom. 3:25; 8:1-8; Col. 3:12-14; Heb. 2:17.
Justification: Rom. 3:19-24; 4:4-5; 5:1-11; Titus 2:11-14; 3:4-7.
Reconciliation: John 15:14-16; Rom. 5:8-10; Eph. 2:11-18.
Regeneration: 2 Cor. 5:17; Gal. 5:16-24; Eph. 2:4-5; 4:22-24; Col. 3:5-17.

   As we become increasingly aware of the battle within us between the Spirit and the flesh; as we identify false beliefs that prompt sinful behavior, and then renew our minds with the truth of God's Word, we can confidently ask God to remove our sinful patterns of behavior, and begin to live in His resurrection power. It is true that we will never be sinless until we reign with Him in His kingdom, but as we grow in Him, we *will* sin *less.*

STEP EIGHT

We make a list of all persons we have harmed,
and become willing to make amends to them all.

And just as you want men to treat you, treat them in the same way. (Luke 6:31)

If we are to make further progress in our journey to recovery, we must prepare to eliminate the burden of unnecessary baggage we are still carrying: the guilt, fear, and shame that either prompts us to avoid certain people or causes us to feel uncomfortable around them.

Many of us experience great anxiety when faced with step 8 because our minds are already racing to step 9, where we actually begin to make amends. However, step 8 precedes step 9 for a reason. Just as in everything else about recovery, so it is here that we will take one thing at a time. *The purpose of step 8 is simply to identify those we harmed as a result of our addiction, and improve our understanding of the responsibility we have in our relationship with them.*

One of these responsibilities is forgiveness. We know that we have been forgiven by God, and step 5 taught us the value of being accepted by another human being. In step 8, we will examine the practice of forgiving other people by preparing to ask *them* to forgive *us.*

Some of us will want to escape this responsibility on the basis that our inappropriate response to someone else was just giving him or her what was deserved. We let someone down because he or she let us down. We didn't pay our fine for a speeding ticket because the police officer was "such a jerk." We broke a written contract because someone in the other party offended us. Or, we may try to justify wrongful behavior because we think we deserved something we weren't going to get otherwise. Theft is often justified this way. We work hard, feel that we deserve a raise, a promotion, or both, don't get what we're after, and take matters into our own hands. We slander the coworker who got the promotion we wanted. Or we steal money, time, or the use of our employer's equipment because we think we deserve it.

Paul wrote these words to the Roman Christians of the early Church:

Never pay back evil for evil to anyone. Respect what is right in the sight of all men.
If possible, so far as it depends on you, be at peace with all men.
Never take your own revenge, beloved, but leave room for the wrath of God, for it is written, "Vengeance is Mine, I will repay." says the Lord. (Rom. 12:17-19)

What does it mean to you to be *at peace with all men?*

How would your life be different if you allowed God to take care of your grievances, rather than trying to take revenge on someone else yourself?

Forgiveness

As we mentioned earlier, one of the benefits we experienced in step 5 was acceptance. Once we have gained someone else's acceptance, it is easier to accept and forgive other people. In fact, our ability, to extend grace and forgiveness is directly proportional to the degree we have personally experienced it ourselves.

Unfortunately, many of us continue to harbor feelings of ill will toward one or more people – including ourselves – even after we have experienced the forgiveness of God and other people.

Are there people you don't like to be around?...or whom you can't look in the eye?...or with whom you get angry every time you even *think* of them?

The following exercise is designed to help you extend the forgiveness God has given you to other people.

Read Matt. 18:21-35.

- How great was the debt of the king's servant?

- Was it possible for him ever to repay it?

Likewise, before you trusted Christ, how great was your debt to God for your sin?

- Was it possible for you ever to repay it?

What did the servant ask for?

- What did the king grant Him?

Why was the king's servant so harsh with his fellow servant over such a small debt?

Read Luke 7:36-50 (especially verse 47) and compare it with the parable in Matt. 18:21-35. What is the foundation for being able to love and forgive others?

Read Eph. 4:32 and Col. 3:12-13.

- To what degree are we to forgive others?

- Describe how God has forgiven you:

What are some of the effects people experience when they fail to forgive, e.g., attitudes toward others, opinion of themselves, quality of relationships, etc.?

Do your answers to the above questions correspond to any effects of failing to forgive in your life? In your attitude toward others? Toward yourself? If so, explain:

Is there any particular sin for which you haven't experienced God's forgiveness? If so, what do you need in order to do so?

Being offended by others is a frequent experience in life. We go through periods when it seems that almost everybody is letting us down. We want freedom from being offended but the beat goes on. We are hurt by both our experience of the offense and our reliving of it. In fact, the initial pain of the wrong usually amounts to only a small fraction of the total hurt. After a while, it should become obvious to us that it is impossible to avoid being offended. However, the majority of our pain can be avoided if we will learn to deal with offenses rather than reliving them countless times. Unforgivingness is a sure way to cut the flow of God's power in our lives. In fact, there are a number of negative consequences which often result from failing to forgive others. Before we examine these, let's look at some of the reasons why we may withhold forgiveness:

Reasons for Not Forgiving

We often fail to forgive others (and ourselves) because we don't think it is possible. We forget how God has graciously forgiven all of our sins through Christ's death, and rationalize why we can't forgive. These are some of the countless excuses we make for our unwillingness to forgive ourselves and others.

The offense was too great. Grant's wife had committed adultery, and he was bitter toward her. Her infidelity was too great a sin for him to forgive. But almost two years after the incident, God began to impress Grant with the idea that he should forgive his wife *just as God in Christ also had forgiven him,* completely and willfully. When Grant finally did forgive her, his forgiveness was coupled with a commitment to rebuild his relationship with her so that she would not be compelled to repeat the incident with someone else.

Roger sat shaking with anger as he recalled his wife's rape. His anger was destroying his health and his relationship with his wife. *How could any man, who really is a man, forgive such an act?* he wondered. The transient who had raped his wife had moved on, and in his perversion, had probably forgotten the incident. He was never caught. Continuing to allow the offense to produce bitterness might ultimately do more harm to Roger and his family than the destructive act of the rape.

He (she) won't accept responsibility for the offense. How many people have offended us but won't agree that they were at fault? The offense might be something slight, such as being overlooked at a social event, or something major, such as being emotionally neglected as a child. Having others agree that they've offended us isn't necessary for us to respond properly to their offense.

He (she) isn't truly sorry. John pulled a practical joke on you which caused you to be late for class, and your professor refused to accept your paper because you didn't have it in on time. John does not see anything wrong with a little joke – he's slightly sorry, but he still thinks it was hilarious. Even if John doesn't recognize the pain he's caused you,

you can still extend forgiveness to him through Christ and refuse to hold the offense against him.

He (she) never asked to be forgiven. For whatever reason, the offender never got around to asking you for forgiveness. Are you going to withhold forgiveness until it is requested? Who is suffering, you or the offender? What would God have you do? (Read 1 Cor. 13:5 and Eph. 4:32.)

He (she) will do it again. Candy's husband had been out late every Friday night playing cards for three years. On some nights he didn't come home. "Me? Forgive that jerk?" Candy asked. The Lord said that the number of times we're to forgive is seventy times seven... in other words, regardless of the number of offenses. However, forgiveness does not mean condoning or accepting unacceptable behavior. Some situations calling for forgiveness also require confrontation and/or allowing the offender to experience the consequences of his or her wrongful behavior. For Candy, failing to both forgive and confront her husband will cause her to be the bitter loser.

He (she) did it again. David had been a horrible husband to Mandy. However, after much effort, Mandy had forgiven him for his insensitivity, his greater concern for the guys on his softball team, his lack of affection for the children, and his callous, domineering attitude. Then, David saw how poor his behavior had become. He began to change. His relationship with Mandy started to improve – until he stayed out late again with the guys. He had done it again! One mistake set the whole conflict back in motion.

I don't like him (her). Generally, we don't have a great deal of appreciation for those who have wronged us. In fact, every emotion within us may call for retaliation against the creep! Only when we realize that forgiveness is an act of the will, and not of the emotions, will we choose to forgive those who have hurt us.

He (she) did it deliberately. "He knew what he was doing, and he did it anyway!" George had been swindled out of ten thousand dollars by his "best friend," Hal. It had been a complex scheme which had required precise timing over a period of several months. As George sat stunned, his mind raced through those times he had been generous to Hal. He thought of how much he had loved Hal and had repeatedly trusted him. The swindle had been completely deliberate, and Hal had used him. George had been played for a sucker. Hal must be laughing at him now. Whether the offense was deliberate or not, God still wants George to forgive Hal.

If I forgive the offense, I'll have to treat the offender well. Ben excused his slander of Steve by pointing out how Steve had offended him. He felt justified in destroying Steve's reputation even though most of the things he had said about Steve were lies.

Shirley was cold to Greg, and had been for two weeks. It was her plan to punish Greg because he had offended her. She would forgive him all right – as soon as she was through punishing him.

Someone has to punish him (her). How often do we want God to be merciful to us and yet want Him to skin other people alive? When we don't see them suffer, we take it upon ourselves to be God's hand of vengeance.

Charles was their pastor, but according to Gloria, he had wasted the church's money. Gloria was in charge of the church women's group. She waited patiently for God to nail Charles, but when God didn't do what she thought He should, she just knew she was the divining rod for Charlie's back. Soon the church had taken sides – pro-Charles or anti-Charles. The result was that the church disgraced itself by splitting in hatred.

Something keeps me from forgiving. Satan actively promotes unforgivingness. When you attempt to deal with this problem honestly, you may be in for a tremendous spiritual battle, with both confusing and conflicting thoughts and emotions. Don't be surprised if you have to resist the devil at every turn in order to accomplish the task of forgiving the offender. Again, forgiveness is primarily and act of the will, not a warm feeling.

I'll be a hypocrite if I forgive, because I don't feel like forgiving. We often confuse hypocrisy with obedience. We are hypocritical only if we do something for selfish gain. For instance, a hypocrite might be a politician who comes to church in order to get its members to vote for him in the next election, but who despises the church and its people. To forgive as an act of the will in obedience to the Lord's command is true spirituality, not hypocrisy.

I'll forgive, but I won't every forget. If we continue to harbor the memory of an offense, we are only fooling ourselves in thinking we have forgiven the offender, and we will not experience any freedom. In true forgiveness, we give up the right to remember an offense or to bring it up again during arguments. (Note: This does not mean that when we forgive a wrong, we'll never think of it again. But it does mean that we won't relish the memory. Choose to think about things that are true, honorable, right, pure, and lovely [Phil. 4:8].)

I'll forgive, because I have found an excuse for the offense. Hank had been very irresponsible during the early years of his marriage. His wife, Sally, had always been able to forgive him by placing the blame on his mother, who had babied Hank even after he was grown. And yet, Sally was continually angered by Hank and his mother. In fact, her volatile temper was destroying her marriage.

Sally thought that she had forgiven Hank when she had really just excused him. By blaming Hank's mother for his immaturity, she had rationalized his behavior, and had reduced his perception of his offensive actions like this:

ORIGINAL OFFENSE   REDUCED OFFENSE

After reducing the offense, she then forgave it. The problem was that she did not deal with the real offense, but with a distortion of it. Therefore, the real offense remained intact in spite of her efforts at "forgiveness."

When you offend someone, or when someone offends you, do you immediately look for a "reason"? If you do, you may be rationalizing. If you come up with an excuse for the question, *Why did I forgive him (or her)?* Then you have not truly forgiven the offense. You have excused it.

Results of Not Forgiving

Stress: Living with the high level of tension brought by an unforgiving attitude in a relationship can result in a weakening of one's mental resources, emotional difficulties, physical exhaustion, and in some cases, illness.

Self-Inflicted Reinjury: Robert recalled this incident: "As I drove home, flashing into my memory was a guy I played basketball with in college. He was a great antagonist of mine, and was one of the few people I have ever met whom I truly wanted to punch out. I began to remember the unkind things he did to me. Soon, anger started creeping up inside me, and I realized that I had never forgiven him for what he had said and done those many years ago. Each time I would think of him, I would get a knot in my stomach and I'd be preoccupied with feelings of hurt and thoughts of revenge for hours, and sometimes, days." How many times are you reinjuring yourself because past offenses haunt you?

No More Love: "I don't know if I can ever love someone again" is a frequent complaint from those offended by a lover. Our deepest hurts come from those we love. One way we deal with the pain of being offended is simply to withdraw, refusing to love anymore. We often make this unconscious decision when we have not adequately dealt with an offense. We may desperately want to love again, but feel that we are incapable of it. Refusing to experience love and feeling unable to love are both devastating conditions.

Bitterness: Emotions trace their lines on our faces. We think others don't notice what's going on inside, but our anger can be detected by even the casual observer. One person recalled seeing a neighbor go through difficulties in her marriage. Hate created such an impression on her that her face became snarled. She still has an ugly look on her face. Unforgivingness produces ugliness of all sorts.

Perpetual Conflict: A couple, both of whom had been previously married, received counseling several years ago. Having been hurt in their first marriage, they anticipated hurt from their present spouse. At the smallest offense they would each react as if their spouse were about to deliver the final blow. They were constantly on the defensive, protecting themselves from the attacks they imagined their mate would deliver. Having been offended in the past, they anticipated more hurt in the present and future, and reacted in a way that perpetuated the conflict.

Walls That Keep Others Out: Strangely, many of us refuse the love that others want to give us. We often may become anxious and threatened when personal intimacy becomes possible.

Jane hoped and prayed that her husband Frank would come to know the Lord. This, she thought, would allow him to be more loving toward her and their children. One day, Frank accepted Christ and over time, his life began to change. He became interested in Jane, and started spending time with her and the children. He was sensitive and loving. Was it a dream come true? Instead of rejoicing, Jane deeply resented Frank for not changing sooner! *If Frank is able to love us like this now, then he's always had the ability,* she thought. She felt confused and guilty about her anger.

Jane's anger was a defense mechanism to keep distance between Frank and herself. The closer they might get, the more pain she might experience if he reverted to his old ways. She had never truly forgiven Frank, so the bricks of unforgivingness were stacked to form a wall that kept him from getting too close. Hiding behind a wall of unforgivingness is a lonely experience.

Forgiveness Is Not Erasure

The modern idea of forgiveness is to approach an offense with a large eraser and wipe it off the books. God has never forgiven like this. He demanded full payment for each offense. This is the reason for the cross. Beside every offense on our ledger is the blood of Christ, which has paid for our sins in full.

The Christian has a unique capacity to extend forgiveness because he or she can appropriate the forgiveness of the cross. God has forgiven us fully and completely. We, of all people, know what it is like to experience unconditional forgiveness. As a result, we can forgive those around us. Think of it this way: *There is nothing that anyone can do to me (insult me, lie about me, annoy me, etc.) that can compare with what Christ has forgiven me for.* When we compare the offenses of others to our sin of rebellion that Christ has completely forgiven, it puts them in perspective. In Eph. 4:32, Paul writes, *And be kind to one another, tender-hearted, forgiving each other, just as God in Christ also has forgiven you.*

List ten things for which you are glad God in Christ has forgiven you. This will prime you to be willing to forgive all other offenders.

Summary of Reasons for Not Forgiving

1. *The offense was too great.*
2. *He (she) won't accept responsibility for the offense.*
3. *He (she) isn't truly sorry.*
4. *He (she) never asked to be forgiven.*
5. *He (she) will do it again.*
6. *He (she) did it again.*
7. *I don't like him (her).*

8. He (she) did it deliberately.
9. If I forgive the offense, I'll have to treat the offender well.
10. Someone has to punish him (her).
11. Something keeps me from forgiving.
12. I'll be a hypocrite if I forgive, because I don't feel like forgiving.
13. I'll forgive, but I won't ever forget.
14. I have forgiven a lesser offense, after excusing the real offense.

The following exercise will help you to recognize any lack of forgiveness in your life and to extend forgiveness to others as God in Christ has forgiven you.

Offense: Describe in some detail an event which caused you pain.

Persons to Be Forgiven: List everyone who participated in the offense.

Reasons for Not Forgiving: Go through the summary of reasons for not forgiving. Which ones apply?

Act of Forgiving: Choose to forgive, remembering the complete forgiveness you have in Christ.

At the conclusion of the exercise, use the prayer that immediately follows (or use your own) as an exercise of faith for each offense.

Example:

Offense	Persons to Be Forgiven	Reasons for Unforgiveness	Date
My brothers never had anything to do with me.	Harry, Frank	*The offense was too great; they didn't agree that they'd offended me; they never asked me to be forgiven; they'll do it again.*	4-28-89

Dear Lord,
I forgive _____ *for* _____ *(offense) on the basis that God has freely forgiven me and commanded me to forgive others. I have the capacity to do this because Christ has completely forgiven me. I do not excuse this person's offense in any way, nor do I use any excuse for not extending forgiveness. Thank You, Lord Jesus, for enabling me to forgive him (her).*
I also confess that I have sinned by using the following excuses for not forgiving:

Receiving Forgiveness

Having examined the importance of forgiving others, we must now ask, *What have I done to others that merits my seeking* their *forgiveness?* Step 4 has well prepared us for this step by enabling us to see *what* we've done wrong. Now we need to know *whom* we have wronged.

We are not yet ready to make amends with these people. Our task here is simply to list their names. In preparing this list, it may be helpful to use these guidelines, referring to step 4:

- From whom did we cheat or steal?

- What promises and/or confidences did we break (sexual infidelity, lying, sharing, something told to us as a secret) and whom did we hurt or betray?

- For whom did we cause pain by missing family obligations (birthdays, anniversaries) or other special days or commitments?

- What social responsibilities (laws, commitments) did we break or avoid, and who was harmed by this?

- What financial obligations did we avoid or wrongly create, and who was harmed or inconvenienced by our behavior?

- What have we done to harm those with whom we've worked?

- What physical damage – to either property or people – resulted from our drinking or using, and whom did we harm?

- To whom have we neglected to show gratitude?

- Who was victimized by our anger, resentment, blame, or fear?

Example:

	Persons We Have Harmed	How we Harmed Them
1.		
2.		
3.		
4.		

Motivations for Making Amends

There are many benefits we will receive from reconciling ourselves to others by making our amends with them. For one thing, it will release us from the control these people currently have on us. Think about those persons you have been avoiding; those you've been dodging, hoping they won't see you, or those you've been excluding from your circle of friends altogether. Have you ever considered that your guilt and fear are controls which are keeping you from the full enjoyment of life and love God desires for all who know Him?

To make amends is to be released from our relational past. It releases us from the fear of someone finding out something about us that we don't want them to know, a fear that will haunt and control us for the rest of our lives if unconfessed.

Making amends will enable us to enjoy increased fellowship with others; a key factor in our continued recovery. Isolation compelled us to continue drinking or using. Restitution frees us from that bondage.

Finally, as we take action to forgive others and experience their forgiveness, we will be able to forgive ourselves more completely. We will better understand that while our behavior may have been shameful, we as persons are not worthless. Learning how to love and forgive ourselves is a prerequisite for genuinely loving and forgiving others.

Read the Scriptures below and answer the questions that follow:

Therefore, since we have so great a cloud of witnesses surrounding us. Let us also lay aside every encumbrance, and the sin which so easily entangles us, and let us run with endurance the race that is set before us,

fixing our eyes on Jesus, the author and perfector of faith, who for the joy set before Him endured the cross, despising the shame, and has sat down at the right hand of the throne of God. (Heb. 12:1-2)

Do you not know that those who run in a race all run, but only one receives the prize? Run in such a way that you may win. (1 Cor. 9:24)

Understanding that a runner is more likely to win a race by facing forward throughout its duration, how will making amends enable you to be a better runner in the "race" of life?

What do you fear most about making amends?

- Do you think this a realistic fear? Why, or why not?

- Are you willing to lay this encumbrance of fear aside and make amends even though it may be painful to do so?

What possible joys might result from making amends?

To which of these do you most look forward, and why?

STEP NINE

*We make direct amends to such people where possible,
except when doing so will injure them or others.*

*If therefore you are presenting your offering at the altar, and there remember that
your brother has something against you, leave your offering there before the altar, and
go your way; first be reconciled to your brother, and then come and present your
offering.* (Matt. 5:23-24)

We know of some college girls who traveled to Europe for a four-week tour one
summer. All were advised to pack lightly, warned that they couldn't possibly enjoy all
that the trip would offer if they were preoccupied with heavy luggage during the course
of their stay.

All but one took the advice. She packed two heavy suitcases with an array of clothing,
shoes, and handbags for every outfit, and all of her accessories – jewelry, hose, socks,
belts, scarves. In her carry-on were her rollers, hairdryer, curling iron, and makeup. She
was determined to look her best at any and every given moment.

The group moved from one destination to the next every two or three days. The girl's
luggage got in the way. It was heavy. Her friends who had packed lightly for an
enjoyable trip, were burdened by the task of carrying baggage that wasn't even theirs. Not
surprisingly, after two weeks, all but the carry-on was shipped home.

"I didn't care what I looked like any more," the girl said later. "I just got tired of
fooling with all that luggage!"

We are now at the point in recovery where we are willing to forego our appearance –
the way we are perceived by others or want to be perceived by them – to unload our
baggage of secrets. We have come a long way already. We have unloaded our sins to
God. We have admitted them to ourselves and to at least one other person. Now we are
going to go directly to those we have wronged, and seek their forgiveness for the harm
we have caused them.

Direct Amends

In making our amends, we must be *direct*. No anonymous phone calls, letters, or
payments to those we have wronged. In fact, unless extreme geographical logistics
prevent us from doing so, we must go in person. Once we have looked someone squarely
in the eye to confess our wrongdoing, we will be able to look that person and others in
the eye always. Why? Because having gained their respect, we will regain ours. If a
personal interview is absolutely impossible, a phone call is our second choice. One of
our objectives is to open a door for dialogue.

Being direct also means assuming complete responsibility for our wrongs. This is not
an opportunity to go and point the finger at someone else, e.g., "I'm very sorry, but if you
hadn't done what you did..." Nor do we want to diminish our responsibility by blaming a
third party, e.g., "Well, I'll admit to using poor judgment, but if Joe hadn't told me..."

Our point in making amends is not to admit how we were misled, though this may have been the case, but to confess that we had a choice in the matter and made the wrong one.

The story of the prodigal son provides a good illustration for making direct amends. The younger of two brothers had demanded his portion of his father's inheritance. After the father graciously gave the son his share of what was coming to him, the son squandered it. Out of money and in need of a job, the son one day determined that he could return to his father and gain employment from him as a hired hand (see Luke 15:11-24). Here's what he said:

I will get up and go to my father, and will say to him, "Father, I have sinned against heaven, and in your sight..." (Luke 15:18).

The son was not going to send an apology by messenger, but planned to go directly to his father and confess that he had wronged both him and God.

Restitution

Making amends is more than just making apologies. Restitution means setting things back in order, righting our wrongs. So far as this is possible, restitution is our goal. We want to demonstrate not only an acknowledgment of our wrong, but a change of heart resulting in a change of *action*. Whenever our actions demonstrate a positive change of direction, we have truly repented.

Define *restitution:*

Read the following passage:

If a wicked man restores a pledge, pays back what he has taken by robbery, walks by the statues which ensure life without committing iniquity, he will surely live; he shall not die. (Ezek. 33:15).

What does this passage say to you about making restitution with creditors, the government, local law enforcement agencies, or in instances of theft?

Seeing that you may or may not be able to make full restitution with the above persons or agencies, what can you do to show a *willingness* to pay back what you owe to each party you have wronged?

How would the above apply to physical harm you have done to others by way of property damage?

To whom do you need to express gratitude?

• What action – large or small – can accompany your words to show that you really mean what you say?

Indirect Amends

The eighth step states that we will make direct amends to others *where possible*. We are again confronted by something we cannot change: the past. The children we may have wronged during our addiction may now be grown. We cannot go back and erase the poor example we might have been for them or the abuse we might have given them. Nor can we make restitution with persons who have died or who have now moved to places unknown to us.

There are, however, some positive, constructive things we can do in these instances by way of *indirect amends:*

We can learn from our mistakes and apply that knowledge to present and future situations. If someone we wronged has moved or died, we can pay what debts we may owe to one of their survivors or make a charitable donation in their name; we can treat their survivors with a special act of kindness. We can do for other people's children or parents what we wish we'd done for our own, not as an act of guilt, but in love. We can pray for those whom we know are still living, but cannot locate. [1]

These are only a few suggestions. List any others you think of:

Avoiding Injury to Others

There are some situations which call for making **partial restitution.** By this, we mean partial disclosure of your wrongdoing. What situations call for this kind of action? The most obvious is sexual infidelity. Telling your spouse about your sexual escapades could cause him or her severe mental and emotional anguish, and could damage your marital relationship beyond repair. In the same way, exposing the person(s) with whom you committed infidelity could be damaging to *them.* Causing others such pain is both needless and harmful. Our goal in making amends is not to do further damage to others, but to right *our* wrongs.

How can we make restitution in such instances? *First, we can repent.* If we haven't already, we can break off the adulterous relationship(s) and resolve that with God's help, we will remain faithful to our spouse for the rest of our lives (one day at a time). *We can also demonstrate renewed interest toward our spouse,* giving him or her the time and attention he or she deserves from us.

Other situations calling for partial restitution *may* be those which would threaten our family's well-being. This could be the loss of employment or a legal implication which would harm family members, coworkers, or friends. Again, our goal is not to avoid reaping the consequences of our sins, but to demonstrate careful consideration for other people in what we do and don't expose about ourselves and others.

Without knowing your situation in detail, we can't possibly direct you in making a decision about matters such as these. God knows your situation. We advise you to consider the matter with Him in prayer. As you seek His direction, it will be wise for you also to consult with an objective minister or Christian counselor (or perhaps, your sponsor) – someone with whom you can talk candidly and from whom you can expect a godly response.

List the people or circumstances in your life which may call for making **partial amends.** Beside each instance, identify the possible damage that could result from making full disclosure:

Example:

Person or Situation	Damaging Results
1.	
2.	
3.	
4.	
5.	

From the above, in what ways can you demonstrate partial restitution by a change of action:

Example:

Person or Situation	Specific Action
1.	
2.	
3.	
4.	
5.	

Still other situations may call for **delayed restitution.** Of course, we never want to make amends with anyone without first considering what we will say and what actions we can change. But what we are really thinking of here are those instances in which the hurt you have caused someone else is still so recent that any present discussion might end in a broken relationship. In these cases, it *may* be prudent to wait to take action.

Careful, prayerful consideration, combined with wise counsel and timing are all-important in successfully completing step 9.

List the people or circumstances in your life which may call for **delayed amends.** (This may include situations where you still have not resolved your own negative emotions.) Beside each instance, list the possible harm that you could cause by making amends now:

Example:

Person or Situation	Damaging Results
1.	
2.	
3.	
4.	
5.	

Name some things you can do about these situations while you are waiting for the right time to make amends:

Take all of these issues to your sponsor, pastor, or counselor; ask him or her to pray through each one with you, and wait with an *open mind* for God's direction.

For Additional Reflection and Application

If has been our experience that making restitution often brings favorable results. Many are completely disarmed by our willingness to be open and honest, and by our admission of wrongdoing. These people usually respond with gracious appreciation for our desire to right our wrongs and our relationships with them. But this isn't always the case. There are those who will respond in anger, shock, indifference, or hearty disapproval. The fear of such a response – or the experience of it in any instance – should not deter us from completing our errand. We must remember that we cannot control the responses of other people. Scripture tells us that *their* response is not the issue, Rom. 12:18 says, "...so far as it depends on *you,* be at peace with all men."

Action Sheet

Turn back to step 8 where you listed all the persons you have harmed. Rewrite those names, and beside each, list the action you plan to take, the date the action is to be completed (if any), and the result of your interview with him or her.

(Note: This exercise may take weeks or even months to complete as you prayerfully determine your best course of action; the point is to have a reminder of both those you need to make amends with and what you're going to do to demonstrate repentance toward them. This will also serve as a source of encouragement for you when you need courage to face more difficult amends.)

Example:

Person	Action to Be Taken	His or Her Response	Date for Completion
1.			
2.			
3.			
4.			
5.			

STEP TEN

We continue to take personal inventory, and when we are wrong, promptly admit it.

Therefore let him who thinks he stands take heed lest he fall. (1 Cor. 10:12).

When we entered recovery, we were like people who have all the abilities of an athlete, but who are completely out of shape. Since that time, we have been exercising, gaining strength in areas that were formerly weak; areas of the mind, spirit and emotions that may never have received any previous attention at all.

Now our goal is to stay fit. We not only continue the exercises we began in steps 1 through 9, but build upon them so that we can become even more well-conditioned. For this reason, steps 10 through 12 are often called *maintenance steps.*

In step 4, we "cleaned house" with what my have been the first moral inventory of a lifetime. Now we need to learn how to do this on a regular basis. Why?

The clutter of past sins led us into the bondage of addiction. Because of the common root of sin (rebellion), one sin – however distantly related – can be the cause of another.[1] A.W. Tozer wrote: "That part of ourselves that we rescue from the cross may be a very little part of us, but it is likely to be the seat of our spiritual troubles and defeats."[2]

We examined proper motivations for obedience in step 6. Our goal in obedience is not to perform for God, but to cooperate with Him by allowing His Holy Spirit to perform through us. Galatians 5:16 says, *...walk by the Spirit, and you will not carry out the desire of the flesh.*

Jesus promised that Christians would be distinguished from non-Christians by their *fruits,* or by what is produced through their actions (see Matt. 7:15-20).

In order to bear the fruits of the Holy Spirit, and in order to prevent "little" sins from becoming the root of greater troubles, it is imperative that we learn how to take a daily inventory. Before doing this, however, it will be helpful to understand the difference between the Holy Spirit's conviction and guilt.

Guilt vs. Conviction

Perhaps no emotion is more destructive than guilt. It causes a loss of self-respect. It causes the human spirit to wither, and eats away at our personal significance. Guilt is a strong motivator, but it plays on our fears of failure and rejection; therefore, it can never ultimately build, encourage, or inspire us in our desire to live for Christ.

Guilt has a restricted meaning in the New Testament. It refers only to man's condition *prior to salvation.* Only the non-Christian is actually guilty before God. He has transgressed the law of God and must face the consequences. Guilt shakes its fist and says, "You have fallen short and must pay the price. You are personally accountable."

In Rom. 8:1, Paul wrote: *There is therefore now no condemnation for those who are in Christ Jesus.* Our condemnation is removed only through Christ. He took all of our guilt upon Himself when He accepted the penalty for our sins, and suffered the full punishment for all sin. Because of His substitution, we need never face guilt's consequences. We are acquitted and absolved from guilt, free from our sentence of spiritual death.

Many of us have been told that we are still guilty even after we have trusted Christ to pay for our sins. And sadly, we have heard this in churches – places that should be loudly and clearly proclaiming the forgiveness and freedom found in the cross. Perhaps some people think that if they don't use guilt motivation, we won't do anything. Guilt may motivate us for a short while, until we adjust to being properly motivated. But a short period of waiting is well worth the long-term results of grace-oriented, intrinsic motivation.

The love of Christ is powerful. He is worthy of our intense zeal to obey and honor Him. The result of proper motivation is an enduring, deepening commitment to Him and His cause, rather than the prevalent results of guilt motivation: resentment and the desire to escape.

Although Christians are free from guilt, we are still subject to the conviction of sin. Conviction deals with our *behavior,* not our status before God. Conviction is the work of the Holy Spirit. He directs and encourages our spiritual progress by revealing our sins in contrast to the holiness and purity of Christ. Conviction is His way of showing the error of our performance in light of God's standard and truth. His motivation is love, correction, and protection.

Guilt brings depression and despair; conviction leads us to the beautiful realization of God's forgiveness and enables us to experience His love and power.

Perhaps the following summary will better reveal the contrasting purposes and results of guilt and conviction:

Basic Focus:
GUILT focuses on the state of being condemned: *I am unworthy.*
CONVICTION focuses on behavior. *This act is unworthy of Christ and is destructive.*

Primary Concern:
GUILT prompts concern about our loss of self-esteem and wounded self-pride: *What will others think of me?*
CONVICTION causes us to be concerned with the loss of our moment-by-moment communion with God: *This act is destructive to me and interferes with my walk with God.*

Primary Fear:
GUILT produces a fear of punishment: *Now I'm going to get it!*
CONVICTION produces a fear of the destructiveness of the act itself: *This behavior is destructive to me and to others, and it robs me of what God intends for me.*

Agent:
The agent of GUILT is Satan: ...*the god of this world has blinded the minds of the unbelieving, that they might not see the light of the gospel of the glory of Christ* (2 Cor. 4:4).
The agent of CONVICTION is the Holy Spirit: ...*but if by the Spirit you are putting to death the deeds of the body, you will live* (Rom. 8:13).

Behavioral Results:

GUILT leads to depression and more sin: *I am just a low-down, dirty, rotten sinner;* or to rebellion: *I don't care. I'm going to do whatever I want to do.*

CONVICTION leads to repentance, the turning from sin to Christ: Lord, *I agree with You that my sin is wrong and destructive. What do You want me to do?*

Interpersonal Result:

The interpersonal result of GUILT is alienation, a feeling of shame that drives one away from the person who has been wronged: *I can't ever face him again.*

The interpersonal result of CONVICTION is restoration, a desire to remedy the harm done to others: *Father, what would You have me to do to right this wrong and restore the relationship with the one I have offended?*

Personal Result:

GUILT ends in depression and bitterness: *I'm just no good.*

CONVICTION ends in comfort, the realization of forgiveness: *Thank You, Lord, that I am completely forgiven and totally accepted by You!*

Remedy:

The remedy for GUILT is to trust in Christ's substitutionary death to pay for the condemnation of sin.

The remedy for CONVICTION is confession, agreeing with God that our sin is wrong, that Christ has forgiven us, and that our attitude and actions will change.

To complete the following exercise, go back to step four and select four incidents from your personal inventory that have caused you to feel guilty. List for each your *primary concern,* your *primary fear,* the *results guilt had on your behavior* and on *your interpersonal relationships:*

Example:

- INCIDENT:
  - Primary Concern:
  - Primary Fear:
  - Behavioral Results:
  - Interpersonal Results:

Although Christians are no longer subject to condemnation, we will not be free from its destructive power until we learn to distinguish between guilt and conviction. The Holy Spirit wants us to be convinced that we are forgiven, accepted, and loved – totally secure – because of Christ. The Holy Spirit is the *paraclete,* or "one called alongside," to lift us up and encourage us. As a part of His ministry, He faithfully makes us aware of any behavior that does not reflect the characteristics of Christ. He helps us understand both our righteousness before God and the failures in our performance.

Knowing this, how can we deal with feelings of guilt? First, we need to affirm that Christ has forgiven us and has made us judicially righteous before God. Our sins do not bring condemnation, but they are harmful, and they dishonor God. We can confess our sins to God, claim the forgiveness we already have in Christ, and then move on in joy and freedom to honor Him. The following prayer expresses this attitude:

Father, I affirm that I am deeply loved by You, fully pleasing to You, and totally accepted in Your sight. You have made me complete and given me the righteousness of Christ, even though my performance often falls short. Lord, I confess my sins to You. (List them. Be specific.) *I agree with You that these are wrong. Thank You for Your grace and forgiveness. Is there anything I need to return, anyone I need to repay, or anyone to whom I owe an apology. Thank You.*

It is important that we affirm our righteousness in Christ as well as confess our sins. God does not need to be reminded of our right standing in Him, but we do. Therefore, we need to make this prayer a daily experience and let it pervade our thoughts and hearts. As we yield to the gentle prodding of God-given conviction, confess our sins, and affirm our true relationship with Him, we will gradually be shaped and molded so that we may increasingly honor *Him who died and rose again on* [our] *behalf* (2 Cor. 5:15).

Identifying False Belief

One goal in taking a personal inventory is to identify the false beliefs that govern our actions, and learn how to replace them with the truth of God's Word. It is helpful to first recognize where our emotions and actions come from. Jesus said, *Out of the abundance of the heart the mouth speaketh* (Matt. 12:32, KJV). In other words, our communication (which reveals our thoughts, emotions, and the intent of our actions) comes from our heart (our belief system). Because a number of the situations in our lives are interpreted by what we believe, our belief system, *not the situation,* is usually the key to our response! The following diagram illustrates this process:

Situations
⇓
Belief System ⇒ **Thoughts** ⇒ **Emotions** ⇒ **Actions**

In addition to comprising our reactions to immediate events, our emotions are products of our family backgrounds, our past experiences, relationships, and patterns of responses. Many of us come from homes where we were not loved and affirmed as children. We may have learned to repress painful emotions because we didn't want to believe that something was wrong with our families, our source of stability and security. Some of us have become numb, unable to feel either anger or joy, hurt or love. Some of us have developed a habit of forgetting difficult instances and their accompanying pain as defense mechanism. There are many different ways to block pain in our efforts to gain a sense of worth, but we need to begin reversing this trend by finding someone who will encourage us to be honest about our feelings. We can then use our feelings as a gauge to determine if our response to a situation is based on the truth or a lie.

It is important to realize that feelings are neither right nor wrong. They are signals which tell us something about our environment. We need to be honest about our emotions so that they can tell us what we need to know about our perceptions.

When our emotions are painful or distressing, we can ask, *Why am I responding this way? Am I believing a lie? If so, which one?*

Tracing Emotions to Root Beliefs

Let's suppose that someone (Bill) picked you up late, so you are late to work (or school, church, committee meeting). Your response is anger. You can trace that anger back to its root false belief in order to replace it with corresponding truths from the Scriptures or a characteristic of Christ presented in step 3. Here is how it would look:

Situation   (Bill picked you up late. You are late to work.)
⇓

False Belief   ⇒   *Ungodly Thoughts*   ⇒   *Emotions*   ⇒   *Ungodly Actions*

(?)   _____ *Anger*

How do you determine the false belief responsible for your anger? Ask yourself, *Why am I angry? Am I angry because...*

- *I hate to be late (your "certain standard"), and my lateness makes me feel badly about myself?*

(I must meet certain standards...)

- *My boss will be displeased with me because I'm late, and her opinion of me means so much?*

(I must be approved by certain others...)

- *Bill failed by being late to pick me up? It was his fault, that creep!*

(Those who fail are unworthy of love and deserve to be punished.)

- *No matter what I do, something always goes wrong?*

(I am hopeless. I can't change. I'll always be this way.)

Note that the proper response is not, *I'm not angry,* when in fact you are. Denial only compounds our problems; it is not a solution. We need to be honest with the Lord and with ourselves about our feelings.

If the situation in the above example had happened to you, what would your emotion(s) probably have been? Which false belief(s) could you trace it to?

Recent Situations

Think over the past two weeks and list three recent situations in which you have had distressing or painful emotions. Take time to reflect on the following questions about each occasion: What were your emotions? What were your actions? What false belief(s) were you believing?

Example:

- SITUATION:
Emotion(s):
    Ungodly Action(s):
    False Belief(s):

Recurring Situations

What are some recurring situations in which you frequently have painful or distressing emotions? Some of these situations may have appeared in the list above, and perhaps include things like: meeting new people, seeing someone whose clothes or mannerisms are different than yours, preparing for a big exam, being late, mingling at parties, being alone, spending extended periods of time with your parents, entertaining people in your home, having to clean up when your spouse or roommate leaves the dishes dirty, despairing when someone disagrees with you or is disappointed in you; being frustrated by a "flaw" in your appearance. What recurring situations trigger anxiety, anger, fear, sarcasm, withdrawal, nagging, etc.?

List three recurring situations in your life. How do you usually respond? Which false belief is at the root of this response?

Example:

- SITUATION:
Emotion(s):
    Ungodly Action(s):
    False Belief(s):

Reject/Replace

Each time you realize that you are responding to a situation with a negative, painful emotion, stop to ask yourself, *Why?* and trace it back to its root false belief. Being honest about our emotions is crucial in our application of God's Word! Once we become aware of the specific lie that is affecting us, we can then apply God's specific solution from His Word – a process that often occurs best in the context of affirming relationships.

If we are not aware of the specific lie we are believing, we usually attempt to meet our need with any and every biblical truth – knowing that it is true and hoping that it will help. However, if Scripture does not speak powerfully to our specific need, we can become frustrated and disillusioned instead of freed and encouraged.

The following exercise will help you to go beyond tracing your emotions back to their false belief. You will learn how to replace insidious lies with the powerful Word of God, so that your thoughts and actions will increasingly glorify God.

For the next fifteen days, develop a habit in your scheduled activities which could permanently change your life by selecting a specific time and place to complete the following daily inventory. Everything else of value in your life usually happens as a result of scheduling. You have a regular time to eat, to begin the workday, and to rest. Schedule a time to reflect on how you respond to daily situations, the false beliefs contributing to your responses, and ways you can reject those beliefs by replacing them with the truth of God's Word.

Recognize
- Describe your situation.
- Describe your response to the situation: your feelings, thoughts, and actions.

Reject
- Which false belief(s) were you believing?

- *I must meet certain standards to feel good about myself* (fear of failure).
- *I must be approved* (accepted) *by certain others to feel good about myself* (fear of rejection).

- *Those who fail are unworthy of love and deserve to be blamed and condemned* (fear of punishment/propensity to punish others).
- *I am what I am; I cannot change; I am hopeless* (shame).

Replace
- Identify the truth from God's Word that applies to the situation;

- **Justification:** *I am completely forgiven and fully pleasing to God* (Rom.3:19-25; 2 Cor. 5:21).
- **Reconciliation:** *I am totally accepted by God* (Col.1: 19-22).
- **Propitiation:** *I am deeply loved by God* (1 John 4:9-11).
- **Regeneration:** *I am absolutely complete in Christ* (2 Cor 5:17).

Pray
- Take your inventory to the Lord and share it with Him. Thank Him for the truth of His Word and for the insight He has given you to see your situation clearly. Then, ask Him to provide what you need to begin experiencing victory in similar situations in the future.

(Note: In a notebook, insert pages as needed for Days 1-15. Complete the following daily inventory for the next fifteen days.)

Example:

Day _____

Date: _____

SITUATION:

- Feelings:

- Thoughts:

- Actions:

If you were following God's truth(s), identify which from example on pages 154-156, and describe the process by which you applied it to this situation:

Truth:

- Process:

If you were following Satan's lie(s), identify which from the previous example, and explain what your response could be in a similar situation:

- False Belief:

- Appropriate Future Response:

What do you need to help you gain victory over a similar situation in the future:

Take this inventory to the Lord and share it with Him. Thank Him for the truth of His Word and for the insight He has given you to see your situation clearly. Ask Him to provide what you need to gain victory over a similar situation in the future.

STEP ELEVEN

We seek to grow in our relationship with Jesus Christ
through prayer, meditation, and obedience, praying for wisdom
and power to carry out His will.

But if any of you lacks wisdom, let him ask of God, who gives to all men generously and without reproach, and it will be given to him. But let him ask in faith without any doubting, for the one who doubts is like the surf of the sea driven and tossed by the wind.
(James 1:5-6)

Jesus Christ's primary purpose in allowing Himself to be made human, to be made sin, and to be crucified on our behalf was to reconcile us to God. He desires to have a relationship with us. In John 10:1-4, 14, He said:

Truly, truly, I say to you, he who does not enter by the door into the fold of the sheep, but climbs up some other way, he is a thief and a robber.
But he who enters by the door is a shepherd of the sheep.
To him the doorkeeper opens, and the sheep hear his voice, and he calls his own sheep by name, and leads them out.
When he puts forth all his own, he goes before them, and the sheep follow him because they know his voice...
I am the good shepherd; and I know My own, and My own know Me...

In Scripture, Jesus is often described as the *good shepherd,* who is faithful to lead and provide for His *sheep,* those who are His. The point of this passage is clear: We can't hope to follow Jesus unless we know His voice, and we can't distinguish His voice from any other until we have cultivated an intimate relationship with Him. Such a relationship takes time, but God clearly wants it. He has taken the initiative in having a relationship with us:

We love because He first loved us. (1 John 4:19)

By this the love of God was manifested in us, that God has sent His only begotten Son into the world so that we might live through Him.
In this is love, not that we loved God, but that He loved us and sent His Son to be the propitiation for our sins. (1 John 4:9-10)

Not only has God taken the initiative to have a relationship with us, but He has given us the resources we need to enjoy that relationship: His Holy Spirit, His Word (the Scriptures), and prayer.

Prayer is our opportunity to communicate through the Holy Spirit to God. Scripture is God's Word (the final authority on matters of life) communicated through His Spirit to us.

Concerning the Holy Spirit's involvement in our communication with God, Scripture says:

And in the same way the Spirit also helps our weakness; for we do not know how to pray as we should, but the Spirit Himself intercedes for us with groanings too deep for words... (Rom. 8:26).

...for through Him we...have our access in one Spirit to the Father. (Eph. 2:18)

But know this first of all, that no prophecy of Scripture is a matter of one's own interpretation,
for no prophecy was ever made by an act of human will, but men moved by the Holy Spirit spoke from God (2 Pet. 1:20-21).

Prayer

As we have just read, the Holy Spirit intercedes for us in prayer. Some people hold to the premise that this means speaking to God in a *tongue,* or language that may be known only to God. But the Holy Spirit isn't limited in the ways He can speak to God on our behalf. To "pray in the Spirit" is to pray with His guidance and wisdom; with an open mind which allows Him to place on our hearts those people and things we need to speak to God about.

God's Response to Prayer
Some of us are uncomfortable with prayer. We find it difficult to concentrate on conversation with an invisible God with whom we experience no audible dialogue. Perhaps, too, we are disappointed with our prayer lives; frustrated because we can't seem to get any answers. What *is* God's response to prayer?

Read Jer. 29:11-14; 33:2-3.

• Have you been discouraged about praying: Why, or why not?

• In what ways are you encouraged by these passages?

God's Reasons for Prayer
God spoke through the prophet, Isaiah, to tell His people: *It will come to pass that before they call, I will answer; and while they are still speaking, I will hear.* If God is in the process of answering before we call on Him, and if He hears us even before we speak, why should we pray? Does it really make a difference: Let's examine what the Scriptures say:

Read 1 Chron. 16:11; 2 Chron. 7:14; Ps. 50:15; Luke 18:1-8; 1 Pet. 3:12.

• From these passages, why should we pray?
Why do you usually pray?

What kinds of things do you usually ask God for when you pray?

God's Requirements for Prayer

Those of us who feel we are doing God a great service when we pray may be surprised to learn that He has requirements for prayer. After all, doesn't He *want* to hear from us? Isn't He the God of love, who freely accepts us? The answer to those questions is yes, definitely! Yet, God is holy. We hear much about the Lord being "our friend," and this is true. Yet He is also *God*. In His holy righteousness, He has set up some ordinances for approaching Him most effectively, and has told us what He does and doesn't like to see in prayer.

Read Ps. 66:16-20; Matt. 5:23-24; 6:5-15, 2 Cor. 7:9-10; James 1:5-6; 1 John 1:9.

* Give as many requirements for effective prayer as you can find from the passages just read:

* What do these passages say about forgiveness as it affects our relationship with God?

* What, according to these passages, are we to avoid?

* What does Matt. 6:5-15 tell you about God's desire for you to be alone and quiet with Him?

* What are some practical ways you can meet with Him on these terms?

God's Resources for Prayer

As we mentioned already, God has given us His Holy Spirit as our Helper in prayer. He has also given us His Word, another tool we can use for communicating with Him. Sometimes, our lives are in crisis, and we are simply too distraught to pray. On other occasions, we may be filled with so much joy and gratitude that we are beyond words of expression. God's Word holds many promises we can take directly to His throne and claim before Him. The Lord delights in this! When we have asked the Holy Spirit to guide our prayers, and are citing the truths of His Word to Him, we can be sure that we are praying in His will.

The Psalms also are an excellent resource for "praying material." David knew the heights of ecstasy and the lonely depths of despair. The Psalms will be of great help and support to you as you pray. They also provide a marvelous example of what true communication with God can be.

Finally, God has given us His people – other Christians – as supporters in prayer. He truly honors a "network" of prayer (Matt. 18:19).

This does not mean, of course, that we should rely solely on the prayers of others for our needs. God desires for each one of us to be in direct contact with Him at *all* times (Col. 4:2; 1 Thess. 5:17).

Do you have a "prayer network" of believers with whom you can pray?

- Whom can you enlist for prayer support?

- For what reasons might prayer support be helpful to you?

In what practical ways can you incorporate prayer into your daily activities?

Priority of Prayer

Many of us *know* we should be cultivating a personal relationship with God, but we often are so busy – perhaps even in Christian service – that we just don't seem to have time to pray. We may also have this perception that our prayers need to be lengthy to be effective. We will discuss the time element later in this chapter. For now, let's look at the priority Jesus placed on prayer.

Read Mark 1:34-35; 6:45-46; and Luke 5:16.

- Why do you think it was important for God the Son to spend time alone with God the Father?

- What did Jesus do to ensure that He could be alone with His Father?

Read Luke 3:21-22; 6:12-13; 9:28-31; 22:39-46.

- What significant events occurred either while Jesus was praying, or as a result of His prayers?

- What were the results of His prayers regarding these events?

- Why did Jesus tell His disciples to pray?

What practical lessons do you learn from Jesus about prayer?

Read Ps. 5:3; Matt. 6:33; Luke 10:38-43.

- From the passage you just read in Luke, does your life reflect the activity of Martha or the quiet submission of Mary? Explain:

- Do you gain any new insights about service – even Christian service – and its priority with God as it relates to prayer? If so, what are they?
- Do you find any comfort in knowing that God values your time with Him even more than your dutiful service *for* Him? If so, explain:

- What do you learn about prayer from Ps. 5:3?

- How can you incorporate the insights you've gained from "The Priority of Prayer" into your daily life?

Essentials of Prayer

There are many methods and varieties of prayer, and God certainly does not restrict us to any one formula! We should feel free to communicate with Him in the ways we are led by His Spirit. However, for those who may just be getting started, we offer a simple suggestion which is easily remembered by the acronym, **ACTS.**

A - **Adoration:** *Great is the Lord, and greatly to be praised...* (Ps. 48:1).

One woman has well said, "If we could better comprehend the depth of God and His love for us, our throats would ache with praise!"

Adoration is praising God for His virtues: His characteristics and abilities. It is that act be which we state the *He* is the living God; *our* God, who is deserving of our single-minded worship and devotion; that *His* is the name above all others. When we come before the triune Godhead – the Father, Son, and Holy Spirit – we may want to praise each individually, or address them as One collectively. The following is only a partial list of the many attributes possessed by the Trinity; you may want to add to this list or use others. Some form of adoration, however, should be a regular part of our prayer time with God.

Attributes of God the Father

•His *works are great; His thoughts, profound.*	Ps. 92:5
•He is our *strength.*	Ps. 18:1
•He is our *Creator.*	Ps. 139:14; Rev. 4:11
•He is *awesome.*	Ps. 68:35
•He is *faithful.*	Ps. 89:1-2
•He is the *God of all comfort.*	2 Cor. 1:3.
•He is *just.*	Deut. 32:3-4
•He is *mighty.*	Ps. 89:8
•He is our *rock.*	Deut. 32:3-4
•He is our *help.*	Ps. 63:7
•He is the *king eternal, immortal, invisible, the only God.*	1 Tim. 1:17
•He is our *fortress.*	Ps. 59:17
•He is our *refuge.*	Ps. 59:16
•He is *merciful.*	1 Pet. 1:3-5
•He is our *sustainer.*	Is. 46:4
•He will *never leave us or forsake us.*	Deut. 31:6
•He is *powerful.*	Ps. 138:7
•He is our *rescuer.*	Ps. 34:7

•He is our *hiding place*.	Ps. 32:7
•He is *love*.	1 John 4:16
•He is *wise*.	Rom. 16:27
•He is *sovereign*.	Ps. 103:19

Attributes of God the Son

•He is the *Christ* (Messiah).	Matt. 1:1-18
•He is the *Son of God*.	Acts 1:4
•He is our *Lord*.	Jer. 23:5-6; Acts 2:36
•He is our *shepherd*.	Ps. 23:1; John 10:11
•He is our *intercessor*; our *mediator with God*.	Heb. 9:15
•He is our *high priest*.	Heb. 3:1
•He is the *way*, the *truth*, and the *life*.	John 14:6
•He is the *light of the world*.	John 8:12
•He is the *Lamb of God* who takes away the sin of the world.	John 1:29
•He is the *bread of life*.	John 6:35
•He is the *Alpha and the Omega* (the beginning and the end).	Rev. 1:8
•He is our *Wonderful Counselor*.	Is. 9:6
•He is the *Prince of Peace*.	Is. 9:6
•He is the *King of kings* and the *Lord of lords*.	1 Tim. 6:15
•He is our *redeemer*.	Gal. 3:13
•He is the *victor* over death.	1 Cor. 15:53-57; Rev. 7:17
•He is our *ruler*.	Is. 2:4; Mic. 4:1-4; Rev. 12:5
•He is *sovereign*.	1 Tim. 6:15
•He is our *deliverer*.	Gal. 1:3
•He is *Immanuel, God with us*.	Matt. 1:23
•He is our *Savior*.	Titus 1:4
•He is our *healer*.	Ps. 103:3; Acts 9:34
•He is the *radiance of God's glory* and the *exact representation of His nature*.	Heb. 1:3
•He is the *head* of all things.	Col. 1:15-20; 2:10

Attributes of God the Spirit

•He is our *helper*.	John 14:16

155

• He is our *teacher*.	John 14:26
• He is *truth*.	John 14:17
• He is our *convictor*.	John 18:8-11; 13
• He is *greater in us than he* (Satan) *who is in the world*.	1 John 4:4
• He is our *comforter*.	Acts 9:31
• He gives us *hope*.	Rom. 15:13
• He *sanctifies* us.	Rom.15:16
• He brings us *joy*.	1 Thess. 1:6
• He *renews* us.	Titus 3:5
• He is our *intercessor* in prayer.	Rom. 8:26
• He *gives us spiritual gifts*.	1 Cor. 12:4
• He is our *pledge of eternal life* from God.	Eph. 1:13-14
• He is the *source of eternal "fruits."*	Gal. 5:22-23

What attributes on the preceding pages are most meaningful to you, and why?

Write some of these praises to God, e.g., *Lord, I praise you for...*

      C- Confession: *Behold, the Lord's hand is not so short that it cannot save; neither is His ear so dull that it cannot hear. But your iniquities have made a separation between you and your God, and your sins have hidden His face from you, so that He does not hear* (Is. 59:1-2).

By way of review, *confession* does not make us forgiven. Christ's work on the cross has already has already accomplished our need for forgiveness. To *confess* is to agree with God, to acknowledge under the Holy Spirit's leading that we have "missed the mark." In so doing, we become aware of our desperate need for God's intervention in our sinful patterns of behavior; we recognize patterns of behavior that need to be transformed by Him; we see situations that in the future may need to be avoided; we become aware of those we need to make amends to; and we realign our purposes with those of God.

Is there any sinful thought or behavior you need to confess to God right now? If so, what is it?

- Can you identify one or more false beliefs which prompted your sin? If so, list the belief(s):

- Which of God's truths can you substitute for the false belief(s)?

      T - Thanksgiving: *In everything give thanks, for this is God's will for you in Christ Jesus* (1 Thess. 5:18).

There is something to be thankful for in *any* situation. We often miss this truth because the enemy (Satan) is making every effort to call our attention to what we are lacking in life, rather than what we have. But we can give thanks for any or all of the following: [1]

•

- *Spiritual blessings* (answers to prayer, salvation, forgiveness, acceptance)
- *Physical blessings* (sobriety, eyes, ears, health, etc.)
- *Relational blessings* (family, friends, coworkers, etc.)
- *Material blessings* (home, job, money, car, etc.)
- *Intangible blessings* (freedom of speech, freedom of worship, freedom of choice, etc.)

From the above, for what are you most thankful?

Get into the habit of thanking God daily for at least *one* of the blessings listed in each category above.

> S - **Supplication:** *If you abide in Me, and My words abide in you, ask whatever you wish, and it shall be done for you* (John 15:7).

There are two forms of supplication: intercession and petition. *Intercession* is praying on behalf of others; *petition* is asking God to meet our own needs.

- **Intercession:** *Far be it from me that I should sin against the Lord by ceasing to pray for you* (1 Sam. 12:33).

Many of us may be surprised to learn that when we neglect to pray for others, it is *sin* in God's sight. Scripture continually refers to believers as the *body* of Christ (see 1 Cor. 10:16-17; 12:12-27; Eph. 5:29-30). Just as the physical body is dependent on its various parts for survival, so it is in the body of Christ. We need each other. God does not intend for us to do His work alone!

We are therefore commanded to pray for one another, as well as for those in authority and for the "lost," or unbelievers, of the world:

...I urge that entreaties and prayers, petitions and thanksgivings, be made on behalf of all men, for kings and all who are in authority, in order that we may lead a tranquil and quiet life in all godliness and dignity. This is good and acceptable in the sight of God our Savior, who desires all men to be saved and to come to the knowledge of the truth. (1 Tim. 2:1-4)

In addition to those in positions of governing authority, we are told to pray for:

- All the *saints*, or believers (Eph. 6:18; Col. 4:3; James 5:16)
- Believers who are in sin (Gal. 6:1)

157

- Anyone suffering from adversity (Heb. 13:3)
- The sending forth of Christian workers (Matt. 9:38)

We can pray for these people the same blessings for which we are thankful, e.g., *spiritual* blessings (see Eph. 1:17-19), *physical* blessings (health, sobriety), *relational* blessings (support, friendships, family), *material* blessings (jobs, home, money), and *intangible* blessings (safety if they are in another country, for example).

Ask the Holy Spirit to guide you as you answer the following, and beside each name you list, write what you think God might be asking you to pray for:

What political authorities may need your prayers?

Example:

Persons	Requests
1.	
2.	
3.	
4.	
5.	

What family members need your prayers?

Example:

Persons	Requests
1.	
2.	
3.	
4.	
5.	

For what other "saints" (friends, ministers, Sunday school teachers, missionaries, Christians who have fallen into sin, etc.) might God want you to pray?

Example:

Persons	Requests
1.	
2.	
3.	
4.	
5.	

What unbelievers (friends, family members, supervisor, coworkers, neighbors) may need your prayers?

Example:

Persons	Requests

1.	
2.	
3.	
4.	
5.	

Write down today's date:

You have just completed a very practical exercise in praying for other people. By writing down your requests, you have already made them known to God! And, you now have a list to refer back to and pray from. Making a list can be beneficial for two reasons: *it enables us to remember what it is we need to pray for, and it enables us to see God's answers!*

Make it a habit to pray for one person in each of the above categories each day. As you begin to see answers to your prayers, you may want to begin your own "prayer journal" so that you can record the persons who need prayer with your requests and God's answers. This can be a very exciting way to pray!

Name some of the benefits you may personally receive by praying for others:

- **Petition:** *For we do not have a high priest who cannot sympathize with our weaknesses, but one who has been tempted in all things as we are, yet without sin. Let us therefore draw near with confidence to the throne of grace, that we may receive mercy and may find grace to help in time of need* (Heb. 4:15-16).

  If you abide in Me, and My words abide in you, ask whatever you wish, and it shall be done for you (John 15:7).

Many of us have a tendency to approach God with the idea of Santa Claus in mind. We may read a passage like John 15:7, and wonder why we do not get everything we wish – like a boat, or a million dollars, or healing from a spiritual malady. Here, there are several things we must take into account:

When Jesus said the words we now find in John 15:7, He knew that if we would abide in Him – in his Word and in His Spirit – and if we would, by an act of our will and the power of the Holy Spirit, allow our sinful ways to be crucified (Gal. 5:24), we would pray according to His will, with a view not only to *our* best, but to what might be best in God's eyes. Because we often don't initially know what to pray for in this regard, it is wise to pray for a *knowledge of God's will and the power to carry that out*. Certainly, we can and should bring our physical, spiritual, emotional, relational, and material needs before God, remembering that sometimes, His answer is *no,* and sometimes, *wait.*

Read 2 Cor. 12:7-10.

- Are there times when God has said *no* or *wait* to your request(s)? If so, name some of those occasions?

159

- What might God have wanted to teach you through those occasions?

Whether God's answer is *no* or *wait,* we must remember the words He spoke to the prophet, Isaiah: *For My thoughts are not your thoughts, neither are your ways My ways, declares the Lord. For as the heavens are higher than the earth, so are My ways higher than your ways, and My thoughts than your thoughts* (Is. 55:8-9).

God's plan and timing are perfect. As we continue to seek Him and walk with Him, we will continue to realize that he can be trusted.

List some of your physical needs:
- Spiritual needs:
- Emotional needs:
- Relational needs:
- Material needs:

Make it your habit to pray for two of these each day, and then use a separate piece of paper (or journal including intercessory prayers) to record God's answers to you.

Mediation

Having established a foundation for the importance of prayer, we are now ready to examine God's communication with us through His Word. Let's look at a few of the many reasons we need to develop a knowledge of God's Word:

Read Is. 40:8; 55:10-11; 2 Tim. 3:16-17; Heb. 4:12.
- From the above passages, describe some characteristics of God's Word:

Read Matt. 7:17-19 and John 15:10.
- Why did Jesus emphasize the necessity of knowing Scripture?

Read Ps. 119:97-105; Acts 17:11; Rom. 10:17.
- From the above, what are some benefits of knowing Scripture?

What results can God's Word accomplish?
What do these promises mean to you?

Which passage about the attributes of Scripture is most meaningful to you, and why?

Read Ps. 32:8.

- Turn back to the list of personal prayer requests you made on pages 158-159. Are there any for which you are currently seeking guidance from the Scriptures? If so, which one(s)?

Obedience

As we mentioned earlier, we can't hope to be obedient to God without knowing His commands. While our goal in Christian living is not *perfection,* we make *progress* in our relationship with God as we practice obedience to Him in our daily affairs.

And Samuel said, "Has the Lord as much delight in burnt offerings and sacrifices as in obeying the voice of the Lord? Behold, to obey is better than sacrifice, and to heed than the fat of rams. For rebellion is as the sin of divination, and insubordination is as iniquity and idolatry... (1 Sam. 15:22-23)

Jesus Christ has paid for our sins, averted the wrath of God, and made us dear, beloved children of God. He is worthy of our obedience! He is Lord! He truly is excellent and He deserves our affections and our efforts. There are no political causes, persons, material goods, no fame or prestige that can compare to the One who *died and rose again on our behalf* (2 Cor. 5:15). As Christians, we have the unspeakable privilege of representing the King of kings. We can do this effectively – for eternal purposes – only as we allow the Holy Spirit to teach and guide us through prayer and personal Bible study. Let's look at some ways we can make both a part of our daily routine.

Getting Started

Many of us are eager to know the Scriptures. We may even envy those who are able to rattle off verses at the mention of any given topic. Usually, however, our jealousy does not propel us into action. Instead, we are often intimidated by the enormity and sometimes, complexity, of the Scriptures.

The two best tips we can give you for personal study are 1) *Get started* and 2) *Ask the Holy Spirit to teach you and help you understand the passages you are reading.*

There is no best place to start in the Scriptures; anywhere will do. The real key is to read on a regular basis. You may want to start with the book of Matthew and read one chapter each day until you get to Mark, and then continue through the four gospels and the New Testament until you are finished. Then turn to Genesis and read through the Old Testament, or start again with Matthew and reread the New Testament.

There is no need to hurry or rush your way through. The point of reading is learning, not finishing. Why? So you can begin to apply God's truths to your life.

You may want to join a Bible study so that you will have some accountability for reading and studying. Perhaps your church, or one in your area, is offering a "Through the Bible in a Year?" program. Some Bibles offer a format for reading through the Scriptures in a year.

The Bible often becomes more meaningful for us when we have something to look for. The following are suggested ways to study the Bible personally:

- **Find attributes of God:** We have given you some of these already. There are many others. Look for them as you read, and write them down.

- **God's commands:** In order to fulfill God's commands, we must know them. As you read, you may want to ask the Holy Spirit to call your attention to His commands, and then ask God's help to keep them.

- **God's promises:** The Scriptures contain thousands of promises made by God to us. He is faithful. He never breaks one of His promises. Read these and underline in your Bible those that are most meaningful to you. You might even try to memorize some as you go so that you will have them in your memory when you need them.

- **God's warnings:** What warnings from God do you need to read and then heed? Watching for them and absorbing them is another way to effectively study His Word.

- **Word studies:** This is taking a word in one passage, and comparing it to other passages using the same word. An example of this is the word *shepherd* in Psalm 23. How is it used in this passage? How is it used in other Scripture passages? Does it always have the same meaning?

- **Character traits:** Who were the great leaders in the Bible? What were they like? What were their assets? What were their weaknesses? What do you learn from that?

- **Topics for prayer:** The Bible is our best resource for learning how to pray in God's will. What ideas for prayer do you gain from reading? Make a list of these and place them in your prayer journal; pray them back to God.

- **Reasons to love God more:** Scripture tells us that *we love because He first loved us* (1 John 4:19). This is only one of MANY reasons why we can love God. Underline passages which cause you to love God more as you read, and refer back to them in times of difficulty.

- **Asking questions:** Using a topic like the one given above, you may want to personalize your reading by asking, *In what ways has God demonstrated His love to me?* Or, in the case of a word study, *In what ways has God been a shepherd to me?* Or, *Am I acting as a shepherd to God's people?*

- **Commentaries:** Commentaries are very useful for providing background information. For example, if you studied the book of Romans, you might want to know whom specifically Paul was addressing; when the letters were written; what his primary purpose was in writing; where he was as he wrote those letters. This knowledge is very helpful in fully understanding the context of Scripture. We do, however, advise you to first read the Scriptures for yourself, ask the Holy Spirit to show you what He wants you to see, and then turn to a commentary for additional help and insight.

These are a few of the many possibilities for personal study; there are many others. Let your imagination be your guide, but above all else, *get started!*

Making Time for God

Earlier, we mentioned that one of the biggest obstacles to our personal relationship with God is T-I-M-E.

Many of us resist approaching God because we feel like we owe Him a large chunk of our time. We do owe everything to God. But the truth is that He is delighted with any effort we make to spend time with Him, and especially if it means having to say no to something else in order to keep the appointment.

These are some suggestions for pursing time alone with God:

- **Start slowly, but be consistent.** You may want to spend ten minutes with God each day at first. You can read five verses of Scripture, and spend the rest of your time in prayer. The point is: do it *every* day.

- **Make an appointment and keep it.** Set aside one special time each day, reserved specifically for you and God.

- **Find a quiet place.** Take the phone off the hook if necessary.

- **Choose a time when you'll be free of interruptions.**

- **Ask the Holy Spirit for help and guidance.**

Every relationship takes time. God, more than anyone else, knows this. As you continue to grow with Him, you'll find yourself *wanting* to spend more time with Him. And you'll gain a special blessing in knowing that God isn't just everyone else's God, but yours.

STEP TWELVE

Having had a spiritual awakening, we try to carry the message of Christ's grace and restoration power to others who are chemically dependent, and to practice these principles in all of our affairs.

Brethren, even if a man is caught in any trespass, you who are spiritual, restore such a one in a spirit of gentleness; each one looking to yourself, lest you too be tempted.
(Gal. 6:1)

A Spiritual Awakening?

Before we can say we've experienced a spiritual awakening, we must know what this means. Some people may tell you that their spiritual awakening occurred when God spoke to them audibly one evening, or when they saw Jesus standing beside them, encouraging them. There's no need to discount an experience like this; it may be valid. Our God is not so small that we would limit the many possible ways He might choose to reveal Himself or His truths to other people. But we certainly don't need to despair if we haven't also had a "lightning bolt" experience with Him. For many of us, "spiritual awakenings" are far more subtle, much like regaining consciousness after a good night's sleep.

Our spiritual awakening, regardless of how significant or small it may have seemed at the time, began with the realization that we were powerless over our addiction. When we later realized that only God through Jesus Christ could restore us to sanity, we may have had two spiritual awakenings. One was that we needed God; the other, a revelation that most – if not all – of our actions until that time had been characterized by unsound thinking: insanity.

Having arrived at step 3, we may have placed our trust in Jesus Christ for the first time. Spiritual rebirth isn't the same as spiritual awakening, though the two go hand in hand. Once we receive the Holy Spirit of truth, the number of awakenings we experience will increase – sometimes dramatically and sometimes not. What we are talking about here is a new form of consciousness which may best be measured by looking back at the past.

Answer the following questions:

- How has your willingness to accept blame changed since you started your recovery program?

- Are you better able to see if and when you are at fault? If so, why?

Can you think of past events in which you tried to control or manipulate others? If so, cite two, and describe any changes in your behavior which have occurred since then:

Remembering that our concern is progress, not perfection, look back to step 4, and find three characteristics that have been difficulties for you. Write down those characteristics and show either how your behavior has changed, or how you are making attempts to change.

Example:

• Characteristic:

• Changes:

Read 1 John 1:6-7.

• Are you now walking in *the light*? If so, how can you tell?

Describe any changes you see in your relationships or in your perceptions of other people:

If you have been reading the Scriptures, name one truth or insight you have received from them recently:

If you have answered only one of these questions affirmatively, you have had a "spiritual awakening." If you have answered several of them affirmatively, you are definitely progressing in a new awareness of your thoughts, beliefs, behaviors, and the truths of God. Such awareness, or "light," lays the foundation for change.

Carrying the Message

Having now arrived at step 12, you've undoubtedly met some other chemically dependent people along the way. And in all probability, you've met some who can't wait to share their story of progress in recovery with you. Why is that? People everywhere love to share their success stories, and in fact, such sharing is a demonstration of God's grace in our lives:

Blessed be the God and Father of our Lord Jesus Christ, the Father of all mercies and God of all comfort;
who comforts us in all our affliction so that we may be able to comfort those who are in any affliction with the comfort with which we ourselves are comforted by God.
(2 Cor. 1:3-4)

And we know that God causes all things to work together for good to those who love God, to those who are called according to His purpose. (Rom. 8:28)

God *is* sovereign! He uses our sufferings to teach us how to comfort others – just as He has used the sorrows of others to comfort *us!* What a joy to witness the destruction and pain of addiction being used for someone else's good!

But there are many other benefits of sharing such comfort with others in situations comparable to what ours used to be. It aids our own recovery. Why? Because it causes us to turn our thoughts and interests outward, toward others. When we were drinking or using, remember, our focus was turned selfishly and destructively inward.

Helping others who are now entering recovery also serves as a sharp reminder of our former state when we were still under the compulsion of addiction. Such reminders make us aware of our need for humility (we are only one drink or drug or pill away from relapse!) and propels us into action.

The following Scriptures remind us of our former condition, as well as the necessity of getting and receiving help through others:

For we also once were foolish ourselves, disobedient, deceived, enslaved to various lusts and pleasures, spending our life in malice and envy, hateful, hating one another.
But when the kindness of God our Savior and His love for mankind appeared,
He saved us, not on the basis of deeds which we have done in righteousness, but according to His mercy, by the washing of regeneration and renewing by the Holy Spirit,
whom He poured out upon us richly through Jesus Christ our Savior,
that being justified by His grace we might be made heirs according to the hope of eternal life. (Titus 3:3-7)

Two are better than one because they have a good return for their labor.
For if either of them falls, the one will lift up his companion. But woe to the one who falls when there is not another to lift him up. (Eccles. 4:9-10)

Helping others is, in part, the telling of a story; the story of your progress toward health through the Twelve-Step program. Write down:

How the Twelve-Step program has deepened your faith in Jesus Christ:

How the power of Jesus Christ is transforming your life:
- Emotionally:
- Relationally:
- Spiritually:
- Mentally:
- Physically:

Describe any differences in your behavior that have resulted from identifying false beliefs and replacing them with the truths of God's Word:

Have other people noticed changes or improvements in your behavior? If so, describe some of these changes?

By writing down some of the many changes that have occurred in your life since you entered recovery, you are gathering some good material to share with newcomers. Scripture gives us many helpful hints for successful sharing. Let's look at some of these:

Read Gal. 6:1.

- How would you try to restore a chemically dependent person in a *spirit of gentleness?* Give several possible applications of this instruction:

- What can you do to ensure that helping newcomers won't be the cause of a downfall in your own life? List several possible safeguards:

Read Phil. 1:27; 4:8-9.

- Is our example to others as important as what we say to them? Explain:

As we experience the joys of giving comfort to others who are chemically dependent, and as we mature in our own relationship with God, we will begin to be compelled to share His transforming love and power with those who are outside the program as well. This is the work of the Holy Spirit, yet some of us shy away from this responsibility because we fear rejection. And for good reason! Christ has assured us of being rejected by at least some people when we take a stand for Him.

In John 15:18-25, Jesus said that the reason we are rejected is because, indeed, we are His: *If you belonged to the world, it would love you as its own. As it is, you do not belong to the world, but I have chosen you out of the world. That is why the world hates you* (John 15:19, NIV). Almighty God has chosen us! He has made us new, set us apart, and reconciled us to Himself. We are special and precious to Him, but we should not expect the world to be thrilled with our commitment to Christ.

Sadly, we often forget that we are special and chosen. At times, we wish we belonged to the world. When faced with the choice of being rejected for taking a stand for Christ or going along with the world, we often choose the world. The fear of rejection is too great. But God has given us a solution to the fear of rejection! We no longer have to accept the opinions of others as the basis of our significance. Instead, the love and acceptance of the infinite, Almighty God frees us to live unreservedly for Him. We can step out in faith and lovingly tell people about Christ's offer of forgiveness. Billions of people are waiting to hear His message!

Proclaiming His Excellencies

This exercise explains our privilege and responsibility to be Christ's ambassadors in a lost world. God has set us apart to be the light and salt of the world, and His Spirit enables us to powerfully influence those around us for all eternity. We have the ability to see the world's spiritual poverty through God's eyes and offer to it God's magnificent solution.

According to 1 Pet. 2:9, you are *a chosen people, a royal priesthood, a holy nation,* and *a people belonging to God.* What do these terms mean to you? (Thing of what you've learned already concerning justification, reconciliation, propitiation, and regeneration.)

What is the result of being specifically chosen by God? (See Eph. 2:10 and 1 Pet. 2:9.)

Read Luke 19:10. What was Jesus' goal in coming to earth?

Read Matt. 4:19; 28:18-20. As we yield our lives to Him and the truth of His Word, in what will we inevitably be involved?

Reflect on what Christ has done for you. Make a list of as many things as possible. Then make a parallel list of what was true of you before you trusted in Christ:

Example:

In Christ	Before Christ
1.	
2.	
3.	
4.	
5.	

Do you have a sense of gratitude for what Christ has done for you? Why, or why not?

Read 1 Cor. 6:19-20 and 2 Cor. 5:14-15. How does your perception of what Christ has done for you affect your motivation to communicate the gospel to others?

Do you view your unsaved family and friends as people for whom Christ died and to whom He wants to extend salvation? (John 3:17-18). If not, why?

How does your perception of the lostness of those without Christ affect your desire to share your faith?

To what extent has Satan deceived Christians about the lostness of people? How can you tell?

Read John 17:18; Acts 1:8; Rom. 1:14-16; and 2 Cor. 5:18-20. What is your personal role in evangelism?
Read Eph. 6:19 and 1 Pet. 4:11.

- What do these passages tell you about the Holy Spirit's role in evangelism?

Read Mark 16:15-16; Col. 4:5-6; 2 Tim. 4:2,5; 1 Pet. 3:14-15.

- What do these passages teach you about your responsibility in evangelism?

- In what practical ways can you apply this teaching?

- From Col. 4:5-6, list some characteristics of salt:

Another reason we may hesitate to share Christ with others is that we fear we won't say the right thing. Let's examine how the Scriptures address this problem:

Read Ex. 4:7-12; Is. 50:4; 61:1; Rom. 9:14-16. What do these passages tell you about God's responsibility for the salvation of people?

- How does this help you?

God's heartbeat is for people. This is clearly seen by the life and death of His Son for the world. When we become God's children through Christ, we join in His purpose: to reach a world destined for an eternity without Christ because of their fallen, hardened hearts. People have *exchanged the truth of God for a lie* (Rom. 1:25), and they desperately need others to share the truth with them. A number of Christians ignore the fact that God has called them to the harvest (John 4:35-38). They not only are disobedient, but are missing out on one of the most exciting parts of God's perfect plan for their lives. It is genuinely thrilling to follow Him and allow Him to make us fishers of men.

1. Hart, Larry, "Confronting Chemical Dependency in Your Church," *Mission Journal*, Feb., 1987, p.4.

2. Johnson, Vernon E., *I'll Quit Tomorrow* (San Francisco, CA: Harper & Row, 1980), p.1

3. Spickard, Anderson, M.D., and Barbara R. Thompson, *Dying for a Drink: What You Should Know About Alcoholism* (Waco, TX: Word Books, 1985), p.17.

Step One

1. Springle, Pat, *Codependency*, 2nd ed. Edited by Susan Joiner. (Houston and Dallas, TX: Search Resources, Inc., 1990), p. 23.

2. The American Psychiatric Association, *Diagnostic and Statistical Manual of Mental Disorders*, 3rd Edition, Revised (Washington, DC: The American Psychiatric Association, 1987), adapted from pp. 166-167.

3. Kübler-Ross, Elisabeth, *On Death and Dying* (New York: MacMillan Publishing, 1960).

Step Two

1. McGee, Robert S., Jim Craddock and Pat Springle, *Your Parents and You*. Edited by Susan Joiner (Houston and Dallas, TX: Search Resources, Inc., 1990), adapted from p.9 with permission.

2. Ibid, pp. 191-194.

3. Ibid, pp. 195-197.

4. Ibid, pp. 199-201.

5. Ibid, pp. 203-206.

6.   Ibid. pp. 207-210.

7.   Ibid, pp. 231-236.

Step Three
1.   McGee, Craddock, and Springle, *Your Parents and You*, adapted from pp. 245-272 with permission.

Step Four
1.   Stanley, Charles, *Forgiveness* (Nashville, TN: Oliver-Nelson Books, 1987), p. 16.

2.   Beviss, Mary and Nini Sieck, "Bless Your Heart Each New Day, " Samplers from the Heartland, copyright, 1987.

3.   Ibid.

4.   White, John, *Eros Defiled: The Christian and Sexual Sin* (Downers Grove, IL: InterVarsity Press, 1977), p.10.

Step Six

1.   Springle, Pat, *Codependency*, adapted from pp. 142-143 with permission.   Search Catalog.pdf

2.   Lutzer, Erwin, W., *How to Say No to a Stubborn Habit* (Wheaton, IL: Victor Books, 1979), pp. 21-23.

Step Nine
1.   *The Twelve Steps of Alcoholics Anonymous* (New York: Harper/ Hazledon, 1987), pp. 95-96.

Step Ten
1.   Lutzer, Erwin W., *Living with Your Passions* (Wheaton, IL: Victor Books, 1983),   p. 65.

2.   Ibid, p. 66.

Step Eleven
1.   Lord, Peter M., *The 2959 Plan: A Guide to Communion with God* (Titusville, FL: Agape Ministries, 1976), p. 17.

CPSIA information can be obtained at www.ICGtesting.com
Printed in the USA
BVOW01s0954120913

330939BV00001B/11/P

67128010R00097

Made in the USA
Lexington, KY
02 September 2017